WORLD SHAPERS
A Treasury of Quotes from Great Missionaries

WORLD SHAPERS

A TREASURY OF QUOTES FROM GREAT MISSIONARIES

Compiled by Vinita Hampton & Carol Plueddemann

Harold Shaw Publishers
Wheaton, Illinois

Copyright © 1991 by Harold Shaw Publishers

Compiled by Vinita Hampton and Carol Plueddemann

ISBN 0-87788-946-5

Library of Congress Cataloging-in-Publication Data

World shapers : a treasury of quotes from great missionaries / compiled by Carol Plueddemann and Vinita Hampton.
    p. cm.
  Includes index.
  ISBN 0-87788-946-5
  1. Missions—Quotations, maxims, etc. 2. Missionaries—Quotations. I. Plueddemann, Carol. II. Hampton, Vinita.
BV2067.W77 1991
266—dc20   90-21104
                                      CIP

---

99 98 97

10 9 8 7 6 5 4 3

Contents

Introduction

Someone turns off the lights, and people in the church sanctuary grow quiet and expectant. A woman, or perhaps a husband and wife team, present colorful slides and a prepared story—of life in another culture, and of the gospel struggling to claim hearts and renew lives. It's a Sunday (or Wednesday) night, and First Church, in honor of Missions Week, has asked these missionaries to tell their story.

The words that best describe the missionary experience are the words of missionaries themselves—from their journals, letters, speeches, and memoirs. Only one who has journeyed through the maze of cultural differences and has seen firsthand the power of the gospel in new contexts can give an accurate account. Visitors to a mission station don't stay long enough to understand. News commentators do not see the undercurrents of gospel regeneration. Even biographers are forced to guess as they piece together the scattered components of lives carried out in places and times unfamiliar to most of us.

Some of the missionaries quoted in this book are well-known; some never achieved "fame" in the written-about sense. Most of them lived in historical periods very different from ours. Their language reflects that difference, and some of their terminologies offend us now in a time of heightened consciousness to ethnic and cultural differences. As we hear some of our heroes and heroines refer to "savages," "negroes," and "ignorant heathen," we must remember that they had no semantic alternatives in earlier times.

We have not changed their words. If Livingstone or Carmichael or Carey were on the mission field today, we suppose they would employ the most emancipatory of speech, for they were indeed liberators and respectors of persons in all classes and races. They were also products of their own societies and had specific prejudices and blind spots, as we all do.

We have chosen quotations that reflect lives both difficult and victorious. We have tried our best to show you the real people behind the names we have grown to love and respect. We think that the people we quote would want it that way—revealing the miracle of God's grace in spite of personal inconsistencies and weaknesses. They lived and died for Christ's sake. Their commitment shaped the world for God's glory.

Today, scores of living missionaries are writing new stories in the history of mission work. We thought it best to quote only those men and women whose stories have already been completed; for this reason we have quoted deceased persons only.

Table of Title Abbreviations

ROM	Reform of the Ministry
SA	A Song of Ascents: a spiritual autobiography
SAS	Henry Martyn, Saint and Scholar: First Modern Missionary to the Mohammedans
SEC	The Spontaneous Expansion of the Church
SJP	The Story of Dr. John G. Paton's Thirty Years with South Sea Cannibals
SMP	Student Mission Power
SOA	Shadow of the Almighty: The Life and Testament of Jim Elliot
SOK	Servants of the King
SOM	The Message of the Sermon on the Mount
SS	Sacred Stories: Daily Devotions from the Family of God
STV	The Smoke of a Thousand Villages . . . and Other Stories of Real Life Heroes of the Faith
SW	The Small Woman
TE	The Exile
TF	They Found the Secret
TFS	The Flying Scotsman
TGS	To the Golden Shore: The Life of Adoniram Judson
TJB	The Triumph of John and Betty Stam
TMW	Thinking Missions with Christ: Some Basic Aspects of World-Evangelism, Our Message, Our Motive and Our God
TOM	Frank C. Laubach, Teacher of Millions
TW	The Transparent Woman
TWP	They Were Pilgrims
UC	Uncle Cam: The Story of William Cameron Townsend
UCG	Understanding Church Growth
UK	The Unshakable Kingdom and the Unchanging Person
UV	Unstilled Voices
VFM	T.J. Bach: A Voice for Missions

God's Call

But when God . . . was pleased to reveal his
Son in me so that I might preach him among
the Gentiles, I did not consult any man . . .
but I went immediately . . .
Galatians 1:15-17a

Now get up and stand on your feet. I have
appeared to you to appoint you as a servant
and as a witness . . . to open their eyes and
turn them from darkness to light, and from the
power of Satan to God, so that they may
receive forgiveness of sins and a place among
those who are sanctified by faith in me.
Acts 26:16, 18

The moment that I became a citizen of Heaven I became a foreigner on earth. It is unfortunate that we have adopted such a phrase as "foreign missionaries." We are all missionaries, and we are all pilgrims and strangers, foreigners in this world.—**T.J. Bach**, VFM, 49

Winning souls out there is the same thing as here, only more difficult. The devil comes to one and says, "Why don't you go home? You can save more souls there than here?" But I had received marching orders to go to China and I had to have God to give them as plain to go back.
—**C.T. Studd,** GC, 548

Christ came to give different gifts to different people. Some He made prophets; some He made preachers; some He made teachers. Since I have become a Christian I have thought He has given me the gift of being a *sweeper*. I want to sweep away some of the old difficulties that lie before the missionaries in their efforts to reach our Hindu widows.—**Pandita Ramabai,** HOC, 22

Even if I never should see a native converted, God may design by my patience and continuance in the word to encourage future missionaries.—**Henry Martyn,** ICF, 197

. . . we realize that it is not the call of needy thousands. Rather it is the simple intimation of the prophetic word that there shall be some from every tribe in His presence in the last day and in our hearts we feel that it is pleasing to Him that we should interest ourselves in making an opening into the Auca prison for Christ.—**Nate Saint,** JP, 288

Lord, if it be not Thy will that I should go to the heathen, permit me not to deceive myself; but if otherwise, oh be Thou my Light, my Way, my Refuge. Direct me, O Lord, what I should do, to whom I should apply, and where I should go. If it is not from Thee, I desire not to go one step further.—**Allen Gardiner,** CAG, 7

In 1944 the Lord called me from aviation to Himself, and now he has sent me back to aviation for Himself.—**Nate Saint,** JP, 140

I have a holy awe of the Lord. In a certain sense I am afraid of Him, for when God gives a command He means business; there is no foolishness with Him, and if the plea of love is not sufficient to elicit our obedience, then the Lord has His own methods of dealing with us. He is most gloriously a God of love, but it is a terrible thing to oppose the Ruler of the universe. The fear of the Lord is the beginning of wisdom, and I want to graduate from life's school with honors.—**Robert Savage,** LSM, 14

I have seen, at different times, the smoke of a thousand villages—villages whose people are without Christ, without God, and without hope in the world.—**Robert Moffat,** AHH, 173

I believe that [in] *each generation* God has "called" enough men and women to evangelize all the yet unreached tribes of the earth. . . . everywhere I go, I constantly meet with men and women who say to me, "When I was young I wanted to be a missionary, but I got married instead." Or, "My parents dissuaded me," or some such thing. No, it is not God who does not call. It is *man* who will not respond! —**Isobel Kuhn,** NAA, 224

The sight of the appalling needs of those people in Southern India changed the whole course of my life, and I could not possibly do anything else but go back.—**Dr. Howard Somervell,** MMW, 12

Would that God would make hell so real to us that we cannot rest; heaven so real that we must have men there; Christ so real that our supreme motive and aim shall be to make the Man of Sorrows the Man of Joy by the conversion to Him of many . . .—**J. Hudson Taylor,** GMC, 112

You will not have to worry about an "opening" in the foreign field; usually there are thousands of miles of "opening" and you can take your choice as to where you will establish yourself.—**Robert Savage,** LSM, 33

I ask only justice for a long and neglected race.—**Henry Benjamin Whipple,** SOK, 20

If you would not be willing to live at the side of a colored person in the United States, don't go to Congo.—**Carl K. Becker,** AHM, 148

Perhaps you try to think that you are meant to remain at home and induce others to go. . . . By going yourself you will produce a tenfold more powerful effect.—**Ion Keith-Falconer,** SOK, 203

. . . if God has called you to China or any other place and you are sure in your own heart, let nothing deter you . . . remember it is God who has called you and it is the same as when He called Moses or Samuel.—**Gladys Aylward,** TW, 51

Missionary organizations are fallible. One of Africa's best missionaries was rejected by three Boards. (Like William Carey, he felt, "Go I must, or guilt will rest on my soul.") —an R.P. Wilder, SMP, 33

I thought of all God's people looking out after me with expectation, following me with their wishes and prayers. I thought of the holy angels, some of whom, perhaps, were guarding me on my way; and of God and of Christ approving my course and my mission. Who will go for me? Here am I, send me.—**Henry Martyn,** GM, 245

The command has been to "go," but we have stayed—in body, gifts, prayers and influence. He has asked us to be witnesses unto the uttermost part of the earth. . . . But 99 per cent of Christians have kept puttering around in the homeland.—**Robert Savage,** LSM, 17

As long as I see anything to be done for God, life is worth having; but O how vain and unworthy it is to live for any lower end!—**David Brainerd,** LDB, 190

I questioned in my mind over and over again why some missionaries did not come forward to found [a mission work] in this country. Then the Lord said to me, "Why don't you begin to do this yourself, instead of wishing for others to do it?"—**Pandita Ramabai,** PR, 45

While vast continents are shrouded in darkness . . . the burden of proof lies upon you to show that the circumstances in which God has placed you were meant by God to keep you out of the foreign mission field.—**Ion Keith-Falconer,** SOK, 190

I could not sleep that night . . . Within the very touch of my hand were three young girls dying because there was no woman there to help them. . . . Early in the morning I heard the "tom-tom" beating in the village and it struck terror in

my heart for it was a death message. . . . after much thought
and prayer, I went to my father and mother . . . and told
them that I must go home and study medicine, and come
back to India to help such women.—**Ida Scudder,** DII, 51

It is not necessary that we go to the Scriptures, or to the
ends of the earth, to discover our obligation to the unevan-
gelized. A knowledge of our own hearts should be sufficient to make plain our duty. We know our need of Christ.
How unreasonable, therefore, for us to assume that the
nations living in sin and wretchedness and bondage can
do without Him whom we so much need even in the most
favored Christian lands.—**John R. Mott,** STV, 69

What abundant opportunities women have to be great!
They may never, it is true, be judges, or lawgivers, directly,
and not many may be poets, or painters, or singers; but
all may be *servants*. And what opportunities to serve!
—**Isabella Thoburn,** LIT, 250

My Master calls me to these poor children of His. I have at
best but a few more years to live. It is clear that my place
is not in the old home any longer. . . . I shall go to the Nez
Perces and earn my eternal reward.—**Sue McBeth,** OOB, 147

Cannot the love of Christ carry the missionary where the
slave trade carries the trader?—**David Livingstone,** DL, 46

I wasn't God's first choice for what I've done for China. . . .
I don't know who it was . . . It must have been a man . . . a
well-educated man. I don't know what happened. Perhaps
he died. Perhaps he wasn't willing . . . And God looked

down . . . and saw Gladys Aylward . . . And God said—
"Well, she's *willing!*"—**Gladys Aylward,** TW, 182-183

God's supervision is so blessedly true that at any given
moment . . . whatever we may face we may say, "For this
cause came I unto this hour."—**John Stam,** TJB, 128

It is odd that a million Baptists of the South can furnish
only three men for all China. Odd that with five hundred
preachers in the state of Virginia, we must rely on a Presbyterian to fill a Baptist pulpit [here]. I wonder how these
things look in heaven. They certainly look very queer in
China.—**Lottie Moon,** GGC, 42

The presence of God became unutterably real and blessed,
and I remember . . . stretching myself on the ground and
lying there before Him with unspeakable awe and unspeakable joy. For what service I was accepted I knew not,
but a deep consciousness that I was not my own took
possession of me which has never since been effaced.
—**J. Hudson Taylor,** HTS, 19-20

Voices of Opposition

*"Now, Lord, consider their threats and enable
your servants to speak your word with great
boldness. Stretch out your hand to heal and
perform miraculous signs and wonders
through the name of your holy servant Jesus."
After they prayed, the place where they were
meeting was shaken. And they were all filled
with the Holy Spirit
and spoke the word of God boldly.*
Acts 4:29-31

The man . . . looking at him with a smile that only half concealed his contempt, inquired, "Now, Mr. Morrison, do you really expect that you will make an impression on the idolatry of the Chinese empire?" "No, sir," said Morrison, "but I expect that God will."—of **Robert Morrison**, MHM, 104

Amongst many who sought to deter me, was one dear old
Christian gentleman, whose crowning argument always
was, "The Cannibals! you will be eaten by Cannibals!" At
last I replied, "Mr. Dickson, you are advanced in years
now, and your own prospect is soon to be laid in the grave,
there to be eaten by worms; I confess to you, that if I can
but live and die serving and honouring the Lord Jesus, it
will make no difference to me whether I am eaten by
cannibals or by worms."—**John G. Paton,** SJP, 28

I told this incident to a medical doctor, and he said: "Why,
there is no miracle in *that!* It was just up-to-date hygiene—
giving nature a chance by cleanliness!"

I replied: "Doctor, to me the miracle lay, not in the
poultice, but in God's telling me what to use; and now it
is to me all the more a miracle of prayer, since you say it
was up-to-date hygienic treatment."—**Rosalind Goforth,**
HIK, 79

And people who do not know the Lord ask why in the
world we waste our lives as missionaries. They forget that
they too are expending their lives. . . . and when the bubble
has burst they will have nothing of eternal significance to
show for the years they have wasted.—**Nate Saint,** JP, 158

I know enough about Satan to realize that he will have all
his weapons ready for determined opposition. He would
be a missionary simpleton who expected plain sailing in
any work of God.—**James O. Fraser,** POF, 10

Only a scattered few people were enthusiastic about this
"impossible venture of faith to use radio on the foreign

fields." Such questions as these were asked: "Would God prosper this new-fangled fad since it operated in the very realm of Satan—the air? Didn't the Scriptures clearly portray the devil as 'the prince of the power of the air'— And didn't radio use the air?" By such argument did many dismiss as hopeless the idea of gospel broadcasting. —**Clarence W. Jones,** RNM, 19

There should be a law against the wholesale sacrifice of life which is continually chronicled amongst those who imagine they are "called" to labor in the unhealthy climes as the wives of missionaries. . . .—from *The Boston Evening Transcript*, regarding Emily Judson, MFL, 41

Had I cared for the comments of people, I should never have been a Missionary . . . —**C.T. Studd,** CAP, 196

Protestant zealots find we transport Catholic missionaries in our airplanes and . . . cut off contributions, saying we're helping promote Catholic missions. Catholic prelates who don't know us personally object because we aren't Catholics and don't tell the tribesmen, whom we help spiritually through the Bible, that they should join the Catholic Church . . . —**William Cameron Townsend,** UC, 204

We visited sixty-six islands and landed eighty-one times, wading, swimming, etc.; all most friendly and delightful; only two arrows shot at us, and only one went near—so much for *savages*. I wonder what people ought to call sandalwood traders and slave masters if they call my Melanesians savages.—**John Coleridge Patteson,** SOK, 181

Many attempts were made by some illminded persons of
the white people to prejudice them [the Indians] against
or fright them from Christianity. They sometimes told
them the Indians were well enough already; that there was
no need of all this noise about Christianity; that, if they
were Christians, they would be in no safer or happier state
than they were in already. Sometimes they told them that
I was a knave, a deceiver, and the like; that I daily taught
them a number of lies, and had no other design but to
impose upon them.—**David Brainerd,** JDB, 66

Those who diligently and impartially read Sanskrit literature, in the original, cannot fail to recognize the lawgiver,
Manu, as one of those hundreds who have done their best
to make woman a hateful being in the world's eye.
—**Pandita Ramabai,** WWE, 59

Young men, you will never see the Soudan; your
children will never see the Soudan; your grandchildren
may.—head of Methodist Mission in West Africa to
Rowland Bingham and companions, 1893, JIJ, 296

Not one voice is heard saying, "I wish you good luck in
the name of the Lord."—**Henry Martyn,** MHM, 15

Remember the miller's donkey. . . . the miller, son and
donkey went to the market. The miller rode the donkey all
the way and people exclaimed, "Cruel man, riding himself
and making his son walk." So he got down and his son
rode; then people slanged, "What a lazy son for riding
while poor old father walks." Then both father and son
rode, and people then said, "Cruelty to animals, poor
donkey." So they got down and carried the donkey on a

pole, but folks said, "Here are two asses carrying another ass." Then all three walked and people said, "What fools to have a donkey and not ride it." So let's go ahead with our work for God and not care what folks say.—**C.T. Studd,** FAF, 29-30

You're right. They [the Indians] have had too much religion. But they have never had the Bible in their own tongue . . .—**William Cameron Townsend,** UC, 75

Young man, sit down: when God pleases to convert the heathen, he will do it without your aid or mine.—said to a young **William Carey,** WCM, 63

If any ask what success I meet with among the natives?— tell them to look at Otaheite, where the missionaries labored nearly twenty years, and not meeting with slightest success, began to be neglected by all the Christian world . . . Tell them to look at Bengal also, where Dr. Thomas has been laboring seventeen years . . . before the first convert, Krishno, was Baptized. When a few converts are made, things move on. But it requires a much longer time than I have been here, to make an impression . . . —**Adoniram Judson,** MFL, 53

Mr. C. thought it a most improper step for me to leave the University to preach to the ignorant heathen, which any person could do, and that I ought rather to improve the opportunity of acquiring human learning.—**Henry Martyn,** SAS, 68

For five years we never went outside our doors without a volley of curses from our neighbours.—**C.T. Studd,** CAP, 95

There are many who regard us as possessed of a strange delusion, many who count us carried away by some fanatical madness . . .—**Robert Speer,** JIJ, 274

We need to look resolutely away from the impossibilities and *to the Lord*. His help will come, though often it cannot break through to us until the last moment.—**Isobel Kuhn,** ITA, 11

Commitment

I am obligated both to Greeks and non-Greeks,
both to the wise and the foolish. That is why I
am so eager to preach the gospel also to you
who are at Rome. I am not ashamed of the
gospel, because it is the power of God for the
salvation of everyone who believes: first for the
Jew, then for the Gentile. For in the gospel a
righteousness from God is revealed,
a righteousness that is by faith
from first to last, just as it is written:
"The righteous will live by faith."
Romans 1:14-17

Oh, that I had a thousand lives, and a thousand bodies! All of them should be devoted to no other employment but to preach Christ to these degraded, despised, yet beloved mortals.—**Robert Moffat,** RMK, 31

I would rather die now than to live a life of oblivious ease in so sick a world.—**Nate Saint,** AYO, 45

I hope you will be a missionary wherever your lot is cast . . . for it makes but little difference after all where we spend these few fleeting years, if they are only spent for the glory of God. Be assured there is nothing else worth living for!—**Elizabeth Freeman,** MFM, 181

But whenever I can say, "Thy will be done, teach me to do thy will, O God, for thou art my God"; it is like throwing ballast out of an air-balloon—my soul ascends immediately, and light and happiness shine around me.—**Henry Martyn,** GM, 239

Life is pitiful, death so familiar, suffering and pain so common, yet I would not be anywhere else. Do not wish me out of this or in any way seek to get me out, for I will not be got out while this trial is on. These are my people, God have [sic] given them to me, and I will live or die with them for Him and His glory.—**Gladys Aylward,** SW, illus.

He is no fool who gives what he cannot keep to gain what he cannot lose.—**Jim Elliot,** SOA, 15

None but women can reach Mohammedan women. . . . So *we* have a solemn duty in this matter that we cannot shift. The blood of souls is on our skirts, and God will demand them at our hands.—missionary wife from Persia, WTH, 65

If these great things are to be achieved we must pay what it costs. What will be the price? Undoubtedly it involves giving ourselves to the study of missionary problems and strategy with all the thoroughness and tirelessness which have characterized the intellectual work of those men who have brought most benefit to mankind. It will cost genuine self-denial.—**John R. Mott,** ICF, 208

My soul longs to feel more of a pilgrim and stranger here below, that nothing may divert me from pressing through the lonely desert, till I arrive at my Father's house.—**David Brainerd,** LDB, 40

The motto of every missionary, whether preacher, printer, or schoolmaster, ought to be *"Devoted for life."*—**Adoniram Judson,** TGS, 409

I have but one passion—it is He, it is He alone. The world is the field, and the field is the world; and henceforth that country shall be my home where I can be most used in winning souls for Christ.—**Nicholaus Ludwig (Count) Zinzendorf,** SMP, 12

I had utterly abandoned myself to Him. . . . Could any choice be as wonderful as His will? Could any place be safer than the center of His will? Did not He assure me by His very Presence that His thoughts toward us are good, and not evil? Death to my own plans and desires was almost deliriously delightful. Everything was laid at His nail-scarred feet, life or death, health or illness, appreciation by others or misunderstanding, success or failure as measured by human standards. Only He Himself mattered.—**V. Raymond Edman,** TF, 150

I can plod; I can persevere in any definite pursuit. To this I owe everything.—**William Carey,** GM, 225

We are constantly amazed at the tremendous medical work being carried on daily at the jungle stations by the missionaries with no medical training. They can't stand by and watch people die so they do what they can.—**Nate Saint,** JP, 209

I am not tired of my work, neither am I tired of the world. Yet when Christ calls me home, I shall go with the gladness of a boy bounding away from his school.—**Adoniram Judson,** TGS, 499

I will open Africa to the gospel or die trying.—**Rowland Bingham,** STV, 13

There are grave difficulties on every hand, and more are looming ahead—*therefore we must go forward.*—**William Carey,** WCM, 183

Recall my period of more than twenty years of service, give me back all its experiences—its shipwrecks, its frequent occasions on the brink of death; give it to me surrounded by savages with spears and clubs; give it to me again with spears flying about me, with the club knocking me to the ground, and I will still be your missionary.—**James Chalmers,** GMT, 149

I want to remind the committee that within six months they will probably hear that one of us is dead. But . . . when that news comes, do not be cast down, but send some one else immediately to take the vacant place.—**Alexander Mackay,** LAM, 21

If Jesus Christ be God and died for me, then no sacrifice can be too great for me to make for Him.—**C.T. Studd,** CCF, 13

The way I see it, we ought to be willing to die. In the military, we were taught that to obtain our objectives we had to be willing to be expendable. Missionaries must face that same expendability.—**Nate Saint,** UV, 17

It may be He has only sent me here as a stopgap. Part of a soldier's duty is to fill gaps, you know. One must as willingly be nothing, as something.—**Amy Carmichael,** ACD, 78

Some will say this is China's war, not ours, but we are missionaries to China and, like the wedding vows, we should be here "for better or for worse, in health and in sickness."—**Nelson Bell,** FDC, 174

To all appearance the present year will be more perilous than any I have seen, but if I live to complete the Persian New Testament, my life after that will be of less importance.—**Henry Martyn,** SAS, 441

I must obey my Master and preach His gospel, regardless of threats or suffering.—**Sadhu Sundar Singh,** MCC, 32

True Charity consists in loving God because he is God, and that it is false love which moves through hope of Paradise or temporal welfare.—**Raymond Lull,** RLI, 144

Whatever can be said of my life and work, at least I have stayed put.—**Robert E. Speer,** MSG, 227

These fourscore and six years serve I Him, and He has never wronged me: how, then, can I blaspheme my King and my Saviour?—**Polycarp,** before his martyrdom, BMS, 35

We did not come to China because missionary work here was either safe or easy, but because He had called us. We did not enter upon our present positions under a guarantee of human protection, but relying on the promise of His presence. The accidents of ease or difficulty, of apparent safety or danger, of man's approval or disapproval, in no wise affect our duty. Should circumstances arise involving us in what may seem special danger, we shall have grace, I trust, to manifest the depth and reality of our confidence in Him, and by faithfulness to our charge to prove that we are followers of the Good Shepherd who did not flee from death itself . . . —**J. Hudson Taylor,** HTS, 181

I have this minute in my control. It is all I really do have to work with; none that went before, none that shall come in the future—only this minute until it has flashed by and gone. . . . It is as magnificent or drab or vile as the thoughts which fill it . . . I fear our most common sin is empty minutes . . . —**Frank Laubach,** TOM, 258

You sons of England, here is the field for your energies. Bring with you your highest education, and your greatest talents. You will find scope for the exercise of them all. You men of God, who have resolved to devote your lives to the cure of souls of men, here is the proper field for you! —**Alexander Mackay,** AHH, 144

Language and Culture

*After this I looked and there before me was a
great multitude that no one could count, from
every nation, tribe, people and language,
standing before the throne and in front of the
Lamb. They were wearing white robes and
were holding palm branches in their hands.
And they cried out in a loud voice:
"Salvation belongs to our God,
Who sits on the throne,
and to the Lamb."*
Revelation 7:9-10

The greatest missionary is the Bible in the mother tongue.
It never needs a furlough, is never considered a foreigner.—**William Cameron Townsend,** STV, 110

It's exhilarating to have a new adventure every day. And when I go to church or to a store, and find here and there a word I can really understand, I feel like shouting. —**Monona Cheney,** GOG, 223

I have many more interruptions than Mr. Judson, as I have the entire management of the family. This I took on myself, for the sake of Mr. Judson's attending more closely to the study of language; yet I have found by a year's experience, that it was the most direct way I could have taken to acquire the language; as I am frequently obliged to speak Burman all day. I can talk and understand others better than Mr. Judson, though he knows more about the nature and construction of the language.—**Ann "Nancy" Judson,** MMJ, 112

Its native people are so backward that large numbers of coolies have been brought in from Chota Nagpur to work on the tea gardens, and Hindus and Mohammedans from the plains have settled there as traders and officials. Over one hundred languages are spoken within its borders, and this babel is a great hindrance to mission work.—**H.P. Thompson,** MMW, 17

During this journey I have been able to make a collection of fifteen hundred new words. There is much sheer hard work to be done before we can hope to do much direct mission work among any of the people. I fully intended to have printed, on my return, the various vocabularies I have collected, but they were all destroyed by fire. I am afraid I felt their loss . . . —**George Grenfell,** PIC, 125

People say that we must adopt the language and culture of the day to be relevant today. That is a mistake. If the

Church marries itself to the spirit of the times, it will be a widow in the next generation. There is a universal language—the language of reality and the language of love. —E. Stanley Jones, SA, 133

His colloquial Turkish was famous, and he knew the folklore, the emotional reactions, the customs, the superstitions, legends and religious beliefs of the common people as few others did.—friend speaking of Lyman MacCallum, CI, 40

... this is their death ceremony, and one who did not enter into it would be regarded as impolite and unsympathetic as someone in the U.S.A. who didn't go to the funeral and look sober. ... We build beautiful coffins and send flowers and light candles ... They play games and sit up all night and sip *wayusa*. —Jim Elliot, SOA, 193

I think I told you of my having translated the Ten Commandments, and sent them down to Underhill where they have a printing press, to be printed there. I am now busy with the Gospel of Mark, but I find it slow work. ..... I find it very difficult to translate many of the ideas which are really of great importance. For instance, I can find no word for "forgiveness" and it has to be translated by "cleansing." "Sanctification" I have not ventured to grapple with yet. Of course at the best in these early days a translation is only an approximation to what it ought to be, but if I can only manage to give the people an idea of the truth I shall be glad.—George Grenfell, PIC, 147

I have been in China more than a year and a half and labored under the delusion hitherto that I both understood and could speak a little of the vernacular. But the jargon which these country women, speaking a slightly different dialect, poured into my ears fairly started the cold sweat, and it was equally appalling to see the vacant stare with which my supposedly choice Pekinese was received by many of the women. . . . and my umbrella now and then proved more interesting than the difference between the true God and the temple idols.—**Luella Miner,** GOG, 19

The Gospel has not yet been preached to them in their own tongue in which they were born. They have heard it only through interpreters . . . who have themselves no just understanding, no real love of the truth. We must not expect the blessing till you are able, from your own lips and in their language, to bring it through their ears into their hearts.—**Mary Moffat,** to her husband, RMK, 67-68

One of the great gaps in child development in Labrador had been the almost entire lack of games. The very first year . . . the absence of dolls had so impressed itself upon us that the second season we had brought out a trunkful. Even then we found later that the dolls were perched high up on the walls as ornaments, just out of reach of the children.—**Wilfred Thomason Grenfell,** ALD, 182

Because the rules of seclusion in *purdah* forbid high-class Indian women folk to go out into public, unless heavily veiled, and bind them to an indoor life, the death-rate from tuberculosis among girls aged fifteen to twenty in Calcutta is six times as high as that of boys of the same age.—**H.P. Thompson,** MMW, 11

Added to the difficulty of learning to speak the language was the greater difficulty of finding terms to express the ideas which the missionary had come halfway round the world to convey.... in many languages the most precious truths of Christianity had to force their way by bending stubborn words to new ideas, and filling old terms with a new content.—**Helen Barrett Montgomery,** WWE, 90

Learning a language and culture through relationships in a community requires a tremendous commitment to the people of the new language.... *If your goal is to live with people, to love and serve them, and to become a belonger in your new community, then learning the language will prove to be a great means to that goal.* And learning the language will probably become quite manageable!—**Tom Brewster,** CML, 4

... the lofty teachings of our Lord—having been fitted to primitive situations—are frequently more readily understood by a jungle Indian than by a cultured person who is a product of twentieth-century civilization.—**Jim Elliot,** SOA, 233

Nearly all had been taught to read and write in Eskimo, though there is no literature in that language to read, except such books as have been translated by the Moravian Brethren. At that time a strict policy of teaching no English had been adopted. Words lacking in the language, like "God," "love," etc., were substituted by German words.... as the Eskimos had never seen a lamb or a sheep either alive or in a picture, the Moravians, in order to offer them an intelligible and appealing simile, had most wisely substituted the kotik, or white seal, for the phrase "the Lamb of God."—**Wilfred Thomason Grenfell,** ALD, 90

Her version and commission was to put the Scriptures into the simplest form of Marathi speech, so that the women of the country with no mental training and a limited vocabulary could easily understand it.—biographer Helen S. Dyer, of **Pandita Ramabai's** translation work, PR, 113-114

The least difficult thing a foreign missionary has to learn is the language; the part of her work which she has the most reason to dread is its responsibility.—**Isabella Thoburn,** LIT, 260

Our language classes with the Catholic brothers are interesting. There is very little grammar study as we discuss our beliefs practically all the time we have together. He hopes to convert me to Catholicism. This week I am writing an article in Spanish on "How to Obtain Salvation" for him to correct and for us to discuss. We carry on most of these discussions in Spanish, so I am at a a disadvantage, but it is vastly worthwhile.—**Robert C. Savage,** RIC, 32-33

When it is considered that the issue of all disputes with the Mohammedans is a reference to the Scriptures, and that the Persian and Arabic are known all over the Mohammedan world, it will be evident that we ought to spare no pains in obtaining good versions in these languages. Hence I look upon my staying here for a time as a duty paramount to every other, and I trust that the Government in India will look upon it in the same light. If they should stop my pay, it would not alter my purpose in the least, but it would be an inconvenience.—**Henry Martyn,** SAS, 440

Americans suffer from mono-lingual myopia—a disease of the tongue that affects the vision.—**Tom Brewster,** ITG, 145

African children must be brought up as Negroes. It is an unforgivable mistake to try to turn them into Frenchmen.—**Charles Lavigerie,** ATA, 136

Strategy

"Let not the wise man boast of his wisdom
or the strong man boast of his strength
or the rich man boast of his riches,
but let him who boasts boast about this:
that he understands and knows me,
that I am the LORD, who exercises kindness,
justice and righteousness on earth,
for in these I delight," declares the LORD.
Jeremiah 9:23-24

Many knights do I see who go to the Holy Land, thinking to conquer it by force of arms. . . . Wherefore it appears to me O Lord that the conquest of that Sacred Land will not be achieved . . . save by love and prayer, and the shedding of tears as well as blood.—**Raymond Lull,** TWP, 171

We decided on a very simple policy: Never meddle in politics, and preach a positive gospel.—**Clarence W. Jones,** CUM, 111

Our hymns reach every woman in the palace, and they are sometimes sung to his highness. We often find that we can sing Christianity to these people when we cannot preach it. This is an opportunity such as no one of our missionaries has had before, of carrying the Gospel into the very heart of native royalty.—**Clara Swain,** EMW, 215

Right strategy tailors mission to fit each of the thousands of separate communities, so that in it the Church may grow.—**Donald McGavran,** WS, 459

Every educated person knows the peculiar position of Hindu women of the upper classes, how they are entirely secluded, and how in their case an ordinary missionary finds no access. But a female missionary who knew something of medical science and practice would readily find access.—**Alexander Duff,** WWE, 125

It would have been impossible for one in foreign dress to go to the places to which I had to go if I were ever to discover the truth about things in India.—**Amy Carmichael,** TF, 39-40

I had a misgiving . . . about ladies wearing the Chinese dress, on this ground: the Chinese despise their own females while they respect foreign ladies; will they treat us with as much respect and shall we have as much weight with them, if we change our dress? But I have found no ground for retaining this misgiving.—**Maria Taylor,** HTM, 157

One or two visits a year were the most that any village could hope for: in between they would relapse into their old beliefs and old ways; no written instructions could be left, for none could read. So instead of the sister going to the villages, the villages must come to the sister. Let one or two chosen women from each come to the centre at Chabua, go through a spell of training there, and return to their villages.—**H.P. Thompson,** MMW, 18

An individual gospel without a social gospel is a soul without a body and a social gospel without an individual gospel is a body without a soul. One is a ghost and the other a corpse.—**E. Stanley Jones,** UK, 40

The best leaders are grown, not grabbed.—**Clarence W. Jones,** CUM, 169

... what is called for is an extended series of factual studies of the effectiveness of missions, the growth of the churches, and the ways in which people have become Christian.—**Donald McGavran,** BG, 153

Christ himself did not heal people in order to break down their prejudices against receiving his teaching. Healing was a part of his message, one of his ways of revealing God to man. Probably he was known as the Great Healer even more widely than as the Great Teacher. And when he sent out his disciples, he sent them to heal as well as to preach.—**H.P. Thompson,** MMW, 65

God grant us faith and courage to keep "hands off" and allow the new garden of the Lord's planting to ripen. —**Lottie Moon,** NLM, 185

We must begin with positive teaching, not with negative prohibitions, and be content to wait and to watch whilst the native Christians slowly recreate their own customs as the Spirit of Christ gradually teaches them . . . —**Roland Allen,** SEC, 79

Proclaim the Word more and argue about it less.—**William Cameron Townsend,** UC, 201

The Christ I presented would be the disentangled Christ— disentangled from being bound up with Western culture and Western forms of Christianity. He would stand in his own right, speaking directly to the needs of persons as persons without any cancelling entanglements.—**E. Stanley Jones,** SS, 145

It may be that decisions which seem to change the character of the work will have to be made. But if the root principles which have governed us from the beginning are held fast, there will be no real change. The river may flow in a new channel, but it will be the same river.—**Amy Carmichael,** TF, 41

If any methods—old or new—can multiply the effectiveness of existing and future reinforced missionary forces on the field to the point where they *can* "cover" much greater territory and larger masses, should not those methods be exploited fully? *Radio* and *aviation* are two *world-covering* methods the twentieth century church has at her disposal.—**Clarence W. Jones,** RNM, 98

The China Inland Mission has appealed for men, single men, to itinerate in sections where it would be almost impossible to take a woman, until more settled work has been commenced. . . . If, after we are out a year or two, we find that the Lord's work would be advanced by our marriage, we need not wait longer.—**John Stam,** TJB, 67

The methods used in the cities won't work. They don't serve the needs of the Indians. . . .—**William Cameron Townsend,** UC, 76

In the beginning of modern missions attention had been concentrated naturally on men and boys . . . There was a certain superiority in the attitude of the masculine world . . . Two generations of hard experience had forced upon missionaries, and through them, upon the Boards at home, the conviction that the citadel of heathendom was in the heathen home, and that this citadel could be taken only by the assault of women. The same Boards whose opposition in the thirties defeated the foundation of [a women's] society, in the sixties were glad to further the organization of the Women's Boards of Missions formed for the purpose of sending out single women to open schools for girls and women.—**Helen Barrett Montgomery,** WWE, 86

You will not alone be curing diseases, but will be battling with epidemics, plagues and pestilences and preventing them. You will be educating people in the laws of health and hygiene; you will be teaching mothers how to nurture their children so that they will make more efficient reliable citizens to take their rightful places in their nation. The practice of medicine affords scope for the exercise of the best faculties of mind and heart.—**Ida Scudder,** address to medical school graduates, DII, 165

Those who would be employed in propagating the Gospel should be familiar with the doctrines he is to combat and the doctrines he is to teach, and acquire a complete knowledge both of the Sacred Scriptures, and of these philosophical and mythological dogmas which form the souls of the Buddhist and Hindoo Systems.—**William Carey,** WCM, 292

It is very unwise to present to the people a one-sided truth—I mean to tell them only of a God of love. They are constantly in bondage of fear because of the evil spirits, and a God of love does not make a strong appeal. They are far more attracted to such truths as the power and greatness of God, the absolute justice of Jehovah and His wrath toward sin.—**Johanna Veenstra,** JON, 125

I am not to expect the Lord to answer in just the way I suggest, or think best. Means and manner and everything must be left to the will of God. . . . He can use anyone, anywhere, with equal ease and freedom.—**John Stam,** TJB, 60

Let's stick to the Bible as our gauge . . . What we know, or think we know, about that Book and the way we live it should not be the mold we pass on to the world, but rather the Book itself.—**William Cameron Townsend,** UC, 121

Prepare for the worst; expect the best, and take what comes.—**Robert E. Speer,** MSG, 69

Discouragement

But he said to me, "My grace is sufficient for
you, for my power is made perfect in
weakness." Therefore I will boast all the more
gladly about my weaknesses, so that
Christ's power may rest on me.
2 Corinthians 12:9

Whom have I in heaven but you?
And earth has nothing I desire besides you.
My flesh and my heart may fail,
but God is the strength of my heart
and my portion forever.
Psalm 73:25-26

Our greatest cause for rejoicing tomorrow will not be that
we have been spared from trial and suffering but that
Christ has been present to sanctify the trials to us and
comfort us in them.—**T.J. Bach,** VFM, 97

Joy and sorrow travel together.—**Malla Moe,** MM, 119

Can we wonder at the mortal weariness and disgust, the sense of wasted powers and the conviction that her life is a failure, that comes over a woman when, instead of the ever-broadening activities she had planned, she finds herself tied down to the petty work of teaching a few girls. —**Lottie Moon,** NLM, 141

God grant that out of the scourging inflicted by the Arabs on this poor country some good may yet arise to those who have suffered so much! Our discouragements are many, but God's kingdom is surely coming, even in this dark, dark land.—**George Grenfell,** PIC, 159

We will never know by experience God's richest blessings of comfort and compassion toward others until we ourselves have had trials.—**T.J. Bach,** PMS, 25

Remember, when you see a missionary coming home broken in body and weary in soul, it isn't the privations or dangers or things he's *done* that leave a deep hurt; it's the things he *couldn't* do that break his heart.—Anonymous, RNM, 100

Within the last twelve months the Lord in His wisdom has seen fit to take from me a beloved child and a tender and affectionate wife. My earthly comforts have been removed, and I pass my days in sorrow. . . . In my deep affliction, He has not left me without mercy and great sources of comfort.—**Allen Gardiner,** CAG, 5-6

We have done very little original work. We have made very few demands upon the brains of the women in our mis-

sionary circles. And as a result, we have been given over
to smallness of vision in our missionary life.—**Helen Barrett Montgomery,** WTH, 143

We are getting along okay although constantly confronted
by little mole-hill mountains . . . as seen through tired
eyes. . . . Even a vacation doesn't do the trick. A fellow
periodically needs to wash his mental hands of the whole
works.—**Nate Saint,** JP, 215

The time may have passed in China when a missionary
has cause to fear personal violence. Yet there remains the
climate with its subtle influence, sapping a man's vitality
almost without his consciousness until he awakens to find
himself a physical wreck.—**Lottie Moon,** NLM, 164

I saw whole Lisu families fleeing, the little children clinging to their mothers' skirts, older folk carrying iron cook-
ing pots, blankets, oil lamps. I stood outside my door and
watched this wholesale evacuation of the people I had
served and loved, mourned and wept over. . . . It seemed
again as though the last twelve months was wasted
labour.—**Lilian Hamer,** EHP, 151

God does most of His work here by bodies half-dead, but
alive in Christ.—**Mary Slessor,** WQO, 157

I live poorly with regard to the comforts of this life; most
of my diet consists of boiled corn. . . . I lodge on a bundle
of straw; my labour is . . . extremely difficult; and I have
little appearance of success to comfort me. . . . *But that which
makes all my difficulties grievous to be borne is, that God hides
his face from me.*—**David Brainerd,** GM, 35

I am still engaged in translation and in compiling the dictionary, which is very laborious work. My courage and perseverance almost fail me . . . This is a very lonely situation . . . I am under continual dread of the arm of the oppressor, and more than that, the natives who assist me are hunted from place to place and sometimes seized. I have been here these ten years now. I feel myself comparatively an old man . . . what a blessing it is to have the hope of eternal life rising brighter and brighter as we enter the valley.—**Robert Morrison,** HOF, 83

My life is lived so much among unlovely and unlovable people that I have learned to have great sympathy and great love for them.—**Eleanor Chestnut,** SOK, 90

Life is hard in White Bay. An outsider visiting there in the spring of the year would come to the conclusion that if nothing further can be done for these people to make a more generous living, they should be encouraged to go elsewhere. The number of cases of tebercle, anaemia, and dyspepsia, of beri-beri and scurvy, all largely attributable to poverty of diet, is very great; and the relative poverty, even compared with that of the countries which I have been privileged to visit, is piteous. The solution of such a problem does not, however, lie in removing a people from their environment, but in trying to make the environment more fit for human habitation.—**Wilfred Thomason Grenfell,** ALD, 103

I have done a great wrong in taking my dear wife into this deadly climate of West Africa.—**George Grenfell,** AHH, 89

I am very defective in all duties. . . . In prayer I wander and am formal. . . . I soon tire; devotion languishes; and I do not walk with God.—**William Carey,** WCM, 162

Sometimes I feel . . . that my cross is heavy beyond endurance . . . My heart seems worn out and bruised beyond repair, and in my deep loneliness I often wish to be gone, but God knows best, and I want to do every ounce of work He wants me to do.—**C.T. Studd,** CAP, 216

. . . that it may be His will to restore me again to you and your parish, with a heart tutored by sickness, to speak more and more as dying to dying.—**Robert Murray M'Cheyne,** TWP, 114

Could we but see the smallest fruit, we could rejoice midst the privations and toils which we bear; but as it is, our hands do often hang down.—**Mary Moffat,** JIJ, 145

It [the murder of his son, Elliott] has been so utterly beyond all understanding and so irreparable that there has been nothing to do except to be quiet and to go on steadily doing moment by moment what needed to be done . . . and simply trust to infinite wisdom and love.—**Robert E. Speer,** MSG, 236

Difficulties are not without their advantages. They are not to unnerve us. They are not to be regarded simply as subjects for discussion nor as grounds for scepticism and pessimism. They are not to cause inaction, but rather to intensify activity. They were made to be overcome. Above all they are to create profound distrust in human plans and energy, and to drive us to God.—**John R. Mott,** ICF, 222

Our hearts are breaking. All our Christians dispersed. We are lonely and deserted, sad and sick.—**Alexander Mackay,** when Christians were being burned alive in Uganda, LAM, 108

I am still weak and not fit for much. . . . I have had five attacks in eight weeks. There is nothing for it but patience.—**Ion Keith-Falconer,** TWP, 186

The saddest thing one meets is the nominal Christian. I had not seen it in Japan where missions are younger. . . . The church here is a "field full of wheat and tares."—**Amy Carmichael,** CTD, 117

For a long time I felt much depressed after preaching the unsearchable riches of Christ to apparently insensible hearts; but now I like to dwell on the love of the great Mediator, for it always warms my own heart, and I know that the gospel is the power of God—the great means which He employs for the regeneration of our ruined world.—**David Livingstone,** DL, 32

If I had not felt certain that every additional trial was ordered by infinite love and mercy, I could not have survived my accumulated sufferings.—**Adoniram Judson,** GMT, 73

Part of the heartache of all missionary work is the bright promising convert who turns out to be a mere puffball,

crumbling like a macaroon under the least pressure.
—**Isobel Kuhn,** GGC, 206

He is helping me to rejoice in our adverse circumstances,
in our poverty, in the retirements from our Mission. All
these difficulties are only platforms for the manifestation
of His grace, power and love.—**J. Hudson Taylor,** HTS, 214

Prayer

---

*"So I say to you: Ask and it will be given to
you; seek and you will find; knock and the
door will be opened to you. For everyone who
asks receives; he who seeks finds; and to him
who knocks the door will be opened."*
Luke 11:9-10

*Do not be anxious about anything, but in
everything, by prayer and petition, with
thanksgiving, present your requests to God.*
Philippians 4:6

I used to think that prayer should have the first place and
teaching the second. I now feel it would be truer to give
prayer the first, second, and third places, and teaching the
fourth.—**James O. Fraser,** IK, 34

My life is one long daily, hourly record of answered prayer. For physical health, for mental overstrain, for guidance given marvelously, for errors and dangers averted, for enmity to the Gospel subdued, for food provided at the exact hour needed, for everything that goes to make up life and my poor service. I can testify, with a full and often wonder-stricken awe, that I believe God answers prayer. —**Mary Slessor,** HIK, 15

While I was praying I noticed that the rapid, hard breathing of the child had ceased. Thinking my darling was gone, I hastened for a light, for it was dark; but on examining the child's face I found that he had sunk into a deep, sound, natural sleep, which lasted most of the night. The following day he was practically well of the dysentery. —**Rosalind Goforth,** HIK, 33

If you are sick, fast and pray; if the language is hard to learn, fast and pray; if the people will not hear you, fast and pray; and if you have nothing to eat, fast and pray. —**Frederik Franson,** MM, 29

The trouble with nearly everybody who prays is that he says "Amen" and runs away before God has a chance to reply. Listening to God is far more important than giving Him your ideas.—**Frank Laubach,** TOM, 120

I learned to worship God anyplace, anytime, walking along the trail or up the mountain.—**Clarence W. Jones,** CUM, 103

The mystery of prayer! There is nothing like it in the natural universe. . . . Marvelous bond of prayer which can span the gulf between the Creator and the creature, the

infinite God and the humblest and most illiterate child!
—**A.B. Simpson,** WCC

Usually when God is going to do a great work, I have
noticed that there is a time of great dearth. Nothing moves.
Nothing happens. All seems so stagnant. These are golden
opportunities for prayer. Our Lord *needs* prayer, and keeps
things from happening, to open space for Himself. And He
is that satisfying portion we need—that food and drink is
Himself.—**Joy Ridderhof,** MS, 153

If you are ever inclined to pray for a missionary, do it at
once, wherever you are. Perhaps she may be in great peril
at the moment. Once I had to deal with a crowd of warlike
men in the compound, and I got strength to face them
because I felt that some one was praying for me just
then.—**Mary Slessor,** WQO, 113

Two of our large wells were quite dried up, and very little
water left in our other two wells. Many of our friends were
praying that God would give us water—and so He did. . . .
More than 1900 people, besides over one hundred cattle
and the buildings that are fast going up, required a great
deal of water. Each of the two wells had all its contents
used up every day; every evening one could see the bottom of the wells, and would wonder where the water
would come from for tomorrow! But there came a fresh
supply in the morning in each well, and it lasted all day.
—**Pandita Ramabai,** PR, 71

Praying without faith is like trying to cut with a blunt
knife—much labour expended to little purpose.—**James
O. Fraser,** POF, 9

Many people like to talk about the great prayer meetings they used to have or about the periods of time and experiences they used to have with God. But today they are too busy to take time to experience these things. We do not depend on the good meals we had years ago for our physical strength today. We must take time to eat every day to maintain our physical strength. Just so, God wants us to take time to talk to Him every day.—**Peter Deyneka,** MPM, 11

Prayer is the core of our day. Take prayer out, and the day would collapse . . . But how can you pray—really pray, I mean—with one against whom you have a grudge or whom you have been discussing critically with another? Try it. You will find it cannot be done.—**Amy Carmichael,** CTD, 199

First, and most important: Go to your work directly from your knees. Do not leave your closet until you feel that God is with you, by His Spirit.—**Sue McBeth,** OOB, 35

. . . a majority of prayers deal either with . . . *stomachs* or *fenders!* Many of our prayers (perhaps 70 percent of them) are for the sick (stomach ailments, appendicitis, emphysema, etc.). Another very common request is, "And get us all safely to our homes following this service" (which means "may we not have any damaged fenders on our nice cars"). Why give the top priority to "stomachs" and "fenders"? Let's put more stress on the spiritual health of our friends, our loved ones, our fellow church members, and ourselves.—**Robert C. Savage,** PP, 19

It is not necessary that we should always know; indeed, perhaps we shall never fully know what any of our prayers wholly mean; God's answer is always larger than our petition, and even when our prayer is most definite and intelligent there is a wide margin which only the Holy Ghost can interpret, and God will fill it up in His infinite wisdom and love.—**A.B. Simpson,** WCC

Brother, if you would enter that Province, you must *go forward on your knees.*—**J. Hudson Taylor,** GOC, 80

I feel the support of prayer. And this is so precious and helpful. No, friends, it is not in vain that you intercede for us! We are not unmindful, but exceedingly grateful! —**Johanna Veenstra,** JON, 181

Pray as Jesus prayed; always make plenty of room for prayer . . . and as He did, do plenty of manual work, for manual work does not mean time taken from prayer, but time given to prayer . . . —**Charles de Foucauld,** ATA, 333

Some people might call this coincidence, but this has happened too often for that. Our staff here has prayed, and the next day it comes—sulfa, aspirin, a load of cement, penicillin. That's the way it's always been. For more than thirty years, we've been living in the midst of a continuing miracle.—**Carl K. Becker,** AHM, 178

Satan will always find you something to do when you ought to be occupied about that [prayer and Bible study], if it is only arranging a window blind.—**J. Hudson Taylor,** HTS, 235

Much prayer much power.—**Peter Deyneka,** MPM, preface

Family

"I tell you the truth," Jesus replied, "no one who has left home or brothers or sisters or mother or father or children or fields for me and the gospel will fail to receive a hundred times as much in this present age (homes, brothers, sisters, mothers, children and fields—and with them, persecutions) and in the age to come, eternal life."
Mark 10:29-30

My Dearest Mary: How I miss you now and the dear children! . . . I see no face now to be compared with the sunburnt one which has so often greeted me with its kind looks. . . . Take the children all around you and kiss them for me. Tell them I have left them for the love of Jesus, and they must love him too, and avoid sin, for that displeases Jesus. I shall be delighted to hear of you all safe in England.—**David Livingstone,** LTP, 75

Thank the Lord for such a pal and companion as Kath, who has entered all along so wholeheartedly into our acceptance of God's challenge for our lives and the plan of radio broadcasting for South America.—**Clarence W. Jones,** CUM, 68

We had planned to leave on a long itinerary of our field as soon as possible after our wee boy had gone; but when I returned home to the empty house, for the first time in more than twenty years empty of children—my heart seemed as if it would break. For two days, instead of preparing for the coming journey, I lay and wept. My dear husband was tenderly sympathetic, but at last in desperation he became stern and insisted on my facing the future and turning my mind to the open door at hand.—**Rosalind Goforth,** CMM, 95

This heavy stroke quite takes the heart out of me. . . . I married her for love, and the longer I lived with her I loved her the more. . . . I shall do my duty still; but it is with a darkened horizon that I set about it.—**David Livingstone,** after his wife's death, MHM, 299

It is my desire to prepare this letter for you, that you may have the latest proof of my affection for you, and earnest desire for your temporal and spiritual welfare. . . . Do not think of entering the gospel ministry unless you conscientiously feel that you are constrained by the love of Christ, and the sincere desire of winning souls to Him.—**Allen Gardiner,** to his son, CAG, 77

The perils of missionary pioneers were shared by the pioneer wives. Judson in his prison, Moffat with the savages in South Africa, Chalmers in the wilderness of New Guinea, Hunt and Calvert in blood-stained Fiji, Paton in the New Hebrides, all these and hundreds more had some woman who stood shoulder to shoulder with them, sharing weariness, danger, loneliness, sickness, death. —**Helen Barrett Montgomery,** WWE, 158

Marriage can be a great blessing or a great curse, depending upon where you place the Cross.—**C.T. Studd,** FAF, 64

There isn't but so much time and the Lord will just have to understand that a mother with little children has to condense her prayers.—**Carie Sydenstricker,** TE, 192

I was totally unprepared to give up my child so soon. . . . The parting was excruciating for me, and for hours afterward I could not sit, lie down or do anything but grieve. I pored over all I would miss in putting her to bed at night, her sweet childish ways, the likelihood she would forget me to some extent—none of the poignant details did I miss. The consequence was that I was fearfully broken up.—**Isobel Kuhn,** ITA, 61

Years later Lottie was asked if she ever considered marriage. "Yes," she said, "but God had first claim on my life, and since the two conflicted, there could be no question about the result."—quoting **Lottie Moon,** STV, 64

Much of this morning taken up in writing to Lydia. . . . May the Lord, in continuance of His lovingkindness to her and me, direct her mind, that if she comes I may consider it as a special gift from God, and not merely permitted by Him. Marshman sat with us in the evening, and as usual was teeming with plans for the propagation of the Gospel. Stayed up till midnight in finishing the letter to Lydia. —**Henry Martyn,** SAS, 175

Oh, to be married to the one you *do* love, and love most tenderly and devotedly . . . that is bliss beyond the power of words to express or imagination conceive. There is no disappointment *there*. And every day as it shows more of the mind of your Beloved, when you have such a treasure as mine, makes you only more proud, more happy, more humbly thankful to the Giver of all good for this best of earthly gifts.—**J. Hudson Taylor,** HTS, 90

How can the child of missionaries, especially pioneer missionaries working on a far and primitive field, get an education? This is the most ticklish of all missionary problems, and feelings run deep and warm on the subject.—**Isobel Kuhn,** GGC, 219

I feel that in being bereft of him, I have not only lost an affectionate husband, but one peculiarly qualified to be a helpmeet in the highest sense.—**Mrs. John Smith,** BMS, 100

Unless you intend your wife to be a true missionary, not merely a wife, home-maker, and friend, *do not join us.* —**J. Hudson Taylor,** GGC, 47

Marj still keeps everything in order and in hand. . . . The Lord surely knew that in this kind of work I would need a partner with a brain like a filing cabinet and one incapable of saying "can't."—**Nate Saint,** JP, 199

About two of our little ones we have no anxiety. They rest in Jesus' bosom. And now, dear brother, though the tears will not be stayed, I do thank God for permitting one so unworthy to take any part in this great work, and do not regret having engaged in it. It is His work, not mine or yours; and yet it is ours—not because we are engaged in it, but because we are His, and one with Him whose work it is.—**J. Hudson Taylor,** HTS, 168

I have offered up three children. I have no more children to give away to God now.—**Carie Sydenstricker,** TE, 198

I think much about you and our little ones . . . I may be home by tomorrow week . . . I have found the people very kind so far. . . . There is no fighting anywhere now, so I feel the "coast" all clear. Kiss the children for me, and tell them to pray for me . . . Good night my dear wife, and God bless you all.—**Thomas Baker,** in last letter to his wife, BMS, 189

If such exquisite delights as we have enjoyed . . . with one another, are allowed to sinful creatures on earth, what must the joys of heaven be?—**Adoniram Judson** to his wife, MFL, 116

Evangelism

Then Jesus came to them and said, "All authority in heaven and on earth has been given to me. Therefore go and make disciples of all nations, baptizing them in the name of the Father and of the Son and of the Holy Spirit, and teaching them to obey everything I have commanded you. And surely I am with you always, to the very end of the age."
Matthew 28:18-20

When I see with what little effort souls can be won, I tremble to think of the many opportunities I am missing. We must do what we can—the little things. God will save them.—**Malla Moe,** MM 172

Those Americans who have a romantic concept of the "noble savage" living a pure and simple existence close to nature should spend a month here. Last week lightning hit one of the houses in a nearby village, and because lightning is regarded as a punishment from the gods, no one even tried to rescue the woman and two children in the hut who burned to death. These, too, are children of God, and they need to know the truth that will set them free for abundant life.—**Don McClure,** AIA, 103

It is sad that such a large part of the missionary movement, dominated by Europe and confused by the rapid changes of the last thirty years, should be so indifferent to the spiritual needs of the Afericasian millions and deaf to the cries of the younger churches to help them evangelize the exploding population of Africa and Latin America. —**Donald McGavran,** CGS, 336

Good spiritual logistics demand that we use *every* means available to us today to reach a lost world that desperately needs Christ.—**Clarence W. Jones,** CUM, 192

. . . when I am gone, say nothing about Dr. Carey, speak about Dr. Carey's Savior.—**William Carey,** LWC, 68

It has been well for me to remember, when speaking to others, that I am a dying man speaking to dying souls. —**T.J. Bach,** PMS, 12

He found over 5,000 men living in camps as they worked on the Greater Winnipeg Water Works, and no Christian witness had been among them for six years. Along the lines of the railway were mining camps, where the people told him he was the first Protestant missionary to visit them in thirteen years. Little wonder that he drove himself and his men to exhaustion as he tried to bridge these enormous geographical gaps.—on a Mr. Henderson, MHV, 33

In China ten out of twelve are illiterate. But a mighty tide has begun to rise. Millions will soon be reading—before we are ready. Are we going to give them reading matter, or who? Will it be clean or not? Will they be flooded with the message of Christ or with atheism? Will they read love or hate? Whatsoever is sown in their minds, the world will reap. . . . That is the most stupendous, the most arresting, the most ominous fact, perhaps on this planet.—**Frank Laubach,** EOT, 80-81

On the human side, evangelistic work on the mission field is like a man going about in a dark, damp valley with a lighted match in his hand, seeking to ignite anything ignitable. . . . here a shrub, there a tree, here a few sticks, there a heap of leaves take fire and give light and warmth long after the kindling match and its bearer have passed on. And this is what God wants to see . . . little patches of fire burning all over the world.—**James O. Fraser,** MR, 144

The conception of one half of the world saved, and the other half lost, the half that is saved going out after the half lost, is a misconception. We are all lost without God. We are not only going to them because they are in need; we need what they can give to us. . . . In the days to come we shall want these men whose hearts have been touched with the grace of God to come and help us in the uncompleted task of evangelization.—**E. Stanley Jones,** CWM, 265

Here are tens of thousands, yea, hundreds of thousands, who never heard of a Saviour. I believe they have not one proper idea of the God we adore. I am about 500 miles from the nearest mission station; and this in a country, as far as we know . . . teeming with population.—**William Threlfall,** BMS, 115

If the children of God had more of the compassion and tears of Christ, there would be more conviction in the hearts of the unsaved.—**T.J. Bach,** PMS, 25

If we believed that Jesus said,
"I'm going to come again,"
We'd see He found us fighting,
Scorning death, disease and pain.

Did we believe that Jesus said,
"I'm going to judge the world,"
We'd certainly see that His banner of love
Was everywhere unfurled.

If we believed that Jesus said,
"Ye are this dark world's light,"
We'd live in the darkest places
To make them sweet and bright.
—**C.T. Studd,** from "Do Ye Now Believe?" QRB, 74

Lado had never seen a missionary, nor had he heard anything of the gospel story, but he felt compelled to travel a hundred miles through enemy country to find, as it turned out, the only white man who could speak his language. This man, Richard Lyth, a devout Christian government official, telling me about it later said, "Lado had never heard the name of Jesus Christ before I talked to him but he was already a believer before he came to me."—**Don McClure,** SS, 132

What are we here for, to have a good time with the Christians or to save sinners?—**Malla Moe,** MM, 132

We are all missionaries. . . . Wherever we go, we either bring people nearer to Christ, or we repel them from Christ. We are working for the great Kingdom of God—the time when all people will turn to Christ as their Leader—and will not be afraid to own him as such.—**Eric Liddell,** TFS, 109

I was inwardly grumbling about lack of opportunity to get out and preach, tied as I was to language study and household duties. "What is that in thine hand?" He asked me. Servants, peddlars who come to the back door. There is always somebody in our hand. Start with them first.
—**Isobel Kuhn,** ATT, 37

We say but little about the idols but hold up Christ crucified. He will draw them away from these vanities. . . . Oh that we may walk humbly before Him, for we have never seen His power on this wise before.—**Jonathan Goforth,** GOC, 110

Our entire work could be revolutionized . . . if we were to major, individually, and collectively . . . in witnessing, in continuous visitation work, in the sort of personal contacts and friendships which result in reproduction and in the making of disciples.—**Kenneth Strachan,** WSA, 110

Every child should be washed. Every child should be educated. The only question is how to get there. The "why's" of life interest chiefly the academic mind. The "how's" interest every one.—**Wilfred Thomason Grenfell,** ALD, 178

I have been a missionary for twenty-seven years, but have never met a heathen tribesman who was looking for salvation . . . they don't know enough to reach out a hand for heavenly aid. Their eyes look not up but down—down on the earth and upon their bodily appetites.—**Isobel Kuhn,** ATT, 54

I tell you, brethren, if mercies and if judgments do not convert you, God has no other arrows in His quiver. —**Robert Murray M'Cheyne,** TWP, 131

It is high time to make known the glad tidings in these dark regions of sin and spiritual bondage.—**Samuel Marsden,** GMT, 97

I have known them to stand listening for hours and night after night, when we ceased preaching to go home, I have heard one hundred to two hundred men cry out "Stay and tell us more!" . . . It is no weariness to the flesh to tell out the Gospel to people so willing to hear. Time flies and our strength is renewed like the eagle's.—**Jonathan Goforth,** GOC, 124

Long, too long has India been made a theme for the visions of poetry and the dreams of romance. . . . One's heart is indeed sickened with the eternal song of its "balmy skies and . . . eternal light"; . . . when above we behold nought but the spiritual gloom of gathering tempest . . . and, underneath, one vast catacomb of immortal souls perishing for lack of knowledge.—**Alexander Duff,** RAD, 101

What Colombia needs is not Christ on their lips, but Christ in their hearts. If religion would save a soul there would be no need of missionaries here, but a religion that is based upon ceremony, images, mechanical worship, and superstition will never avail in bringing to the people of Colombia the peace, certainty, and transforming power that we have in the glorious salvation of our Redeemer, Jesus Christ.—**Robert C. Savage,** RIC, 35

We have all eternity to tell of victories won for Christ, but we have only a few hours before sunset to win them. —Anonymous, GOC, 341

Across that gulf no matter how wide and deep it may be, love can throw its bridges. We must go among the men who live sincerely in the opposite camps, loving them for God's sake and their own. Only so will truth have its way in men's hearts.—**Lyman MacCallum,** CI, 135

Nobody can force a single soul . . . to turn to Christ. All that [we] . . . can do, is to lift up Christ before the world, bring Him into dingy corners and dark places of the earth where He is unknown, introduce Him to strangers, talk about Him to everybody, and live so closely with and in

Him that others may see that there really is such a Person
as Jesus . . . —**Elizabeth "Betty" Stam,** TJB, 126

The harvest here is indeed great, and the laborers are few
and imperfectly fitted, without much grace, for such a
work. And yet grace can make a few feeble instruments
the means of accomplishing great things—things greater
even than we can conceive.—**J. Hudson Taylor,** GMC, 111

Humor

A cheerful heart is good medicine . . .
Proverbs 17:22a

Our mouths were filled with laughter,
Our tongues with songs of joy. . . .
The LORD has done great things for us,
and we are filled with joy.
Psalm 126:2-3

A good thing to have up your sleeve is a sanctified funny-bone.—**C.T. Studd,** FAF, 95

The other day Marghi got up from her afternoon nap and was frightened by meeting a snake in our living room. . . . a yard-long spitting cobra! She yelled for me, and we got it killed without much trouble . . . Unlike our mother Eve, I do not discuss theology with a serpent; I just dispatch them.—**Don McClure,** AIA, 229

It's amazing what can be accomplished if you don't worry about who gets the credit.—**Clarence W. Jones,** CUM, 141

When I get to Heaven they aren't going to see much of me but my heels, for I'll be hanging over the golden wall keeping an eye on the Lisu Church!—**Isobel Kuhn,** IK, 15

Today is my first up and around since the all-night-long attack of diarrhea that left me so weak by 5 a.m. that I could only roll on the floor, calling for help. . . . When lying in your own dung, only semi-conscious, linguistically dumb, please forgive me for not being more explicit on the finances.—**Nate Saint,** JP, 120

God loves a cheerful giver and everyone likes to be loved.—**Malla Moe,** MM, 209

The other night the druggist gave me a prescription which you may find useful, though the ingredients are more difficult to procure in America than in China. You must catch some little rats whose eyes are not yet open, pound them to a jelly, and add lime and peanut oil. Warranted to cure any kind of an ulcer.—**Eleanor Chestnut,** SOK, 103

I can't *stand* these people who are so goody-goody and holy-holy. . . . Eric wasn't like that. His wonderful sense of humour saved him from ever being like that. He had a poker-faced humour, and you had to watch his eyes very carefully. They usually gave him away, if you looked closely.—Florence Liddell, about her husband **Eric Liddell,** TFS, 107

But you're only a girl, and girls can't be missionaries. *I'm* going to be one and you can come out with me, and if you're good I may let you up into my pulpit beside me. —Robert Slessor, brother of **Mary Slessor,** when they were children, WQO, 3

Oh, I sing every day. If I should stop a day, my throat might find out how old I am.—**Charlotte Tucker,** WWE, 183

The intercom whistled and announced that Protestant service was starting in the Mess. . . . About fifteen lads were present. A Catholic lad with accordian was routed out to help with the singing. I am sure it was not sabotage, but from then on I had him to contend with, as well as the hymns to lead. At least he started us on the right note, but from that point onward we rarely caught sight of each other.—**Lyman MacCallum,** CI, 130

I have to perform all my operations now in my bathroom, which was as small as the law allowed before. Now with an operating table it is decidedly full. I do not mind those inconveniences at all, however. I wish I could look forward to as good accommodations for the work next year. —**Eleanor Chestnut,** SOK, 101

Charlie Studd has written me a delightful letter . . . He thinks the Chinese language was invented by the devil to prevent the Chinese from ever hearing the Gospel properly.—**Ion Keith-Falconer,** TWP, 170

. . . and over that side of the island all their sacred men were at work trying to kill me by their arts. Now and again messengers arrived from every quarter of the island, inquiring anxiously after my health, and wondering if I was not feeling sick . . . —**John G. Paton,** SJP, 67

In Harry, [Ken's son], Ken would tolerate nothing but near perfection, and once wrote, "It is just sheer carelessness to mispell words . . . No educated person can afford to mispell words." Harry made a list of three words besides *misspell* which his father had misspelled.—of **Kenneth Strachan,** WSA, 115

The tower of Babel must have been located in or near New Guinea.—**James Chalmers,** GMT, 135

The food of the Chinese poor is different from that of the middle classes, and I did not find it palatable at first. The story of how I learned to eat beancurd is a family joke now. My husband says, with eyes twinkling, "You have to cry first—then you learn to enjoy it!"—**Isobel Kuhn,** ITA, 38

Let the head grow wise, but keep the heart always young and playful.—**David Livingstone,** DL, 67

I hope that by next week we'll move into our third house since we were married—first the tent, then the thatch roof in Puyupunga, and now, boards, concrete, and aluminum! Where does one go from there?—**Jim Elliot,** SOA, 220-221

First there should be a total commitment to God, then to a country, and finally to a mission. Then you must be a specialist in one or two areas, and very good in several others. Bring along a tuxedo to meet the president and overalls to do whatever work comes to hand.—**Clarence W. Jones** and **Reuben Larson,** CTV, 37

Protection and Providence

Find rest, O my soul, in God alone;
my hope comes from him.
He alone is my rock and my salvation;
he is my fortress, I will not be shaken.
My salvation and my honor depend on God;
he is my mighty rock, my refuge.
Trust in him at all times, O people;
pour out your hearts to him,
for God is our refuge.
Psalm 62:5-8

The abiding consciousness of the presence and power of my Saviour preserved me from losing my reason.... I had my nearest and dearest glimpses of the Face and smile of my blessed Lord in those dread moments when musket, club, or spear was being levelled at my life.—**John G. Paton,** SJP, 56

The secret of victory over death—the assurance of immortality—is not an argument of the mind; it is the conviction of the heart. It is reached through faith, by those who trust Christ and experience the love of God by committing their lives to him, accepting his promises, his challenges, and his rebukes.—**Eric Liddell,** DCL, 121

Many times we realized that we, as well as our fellow workers at the other stations, were kept from serious harm only by the overruling, protecting power of God in answer to the many prayers which were going up for us all at this critical juncture in the history of our mission. —**Rosalind Goforth,** HIK, 28

... life is not long enough, nor money plentiful enough, to spend much of either on the clothes we wear.—**Isabella Thoburn,** SOK, 150

After having been so far, and being so kindly received, even in places where hitherto the natives have been hostile to the white man, I cannot but be devoutly grateful for the protection of the Almighty and for His goodness in preparing my way.—**George Grenfell,** PIC, 92

All the depressions and slim months in the world could not keep the Lord from sending us the money we need. . . . What God is doing is giving us a chance to *suffer* and *believe* so that He can work out a more precious and eternal weight of glory. A test isn't a test unless it is a *test!*—**Joy Ridderhof,** MS, 146-147

Safety does not depend on our conception of the absence of danger. Safety is found in God's presence, in the center of His perfect will.—**T.J. Bach,** PMS, 32

I don't think we are in any danger, and if we are, we might as well die suddenly in God's work as by some long-drawn-out illness at home.—**Eleanor Chestnut,** WWE, 198

The safest place for yourself and the children is in the path of duty.—**Jonathan Goforth,** HIK, 83

Thus, on that one trip, we had been graciously delivered, from fire, wreck, and plague!—**Rosalind Goforth,** GOC, 288

Thank God we are safely back! It might have been otherwise, for we have encountered perils not a few. But the winds, which sometimes were simply terrific, and the rocks, which knocked three holes in the steamer as we were running away at night from cannibals, have not wrecked us. We have been attacked by natives about twenty different times, we have been stoned and shot at with arrows, and have been the marks for more spears than we can count.—**George Grenfell,** PIC, 118

For many days thereafter we had to take unusual care, and not unduly expose ourselves to danger; for dark characters were seen prowling about in the bush near at hand, and we knew that our life was the prize. We took what care we could, and God the Lord did the rest; or rather He did all—for His wisdom guided us, and His power baffled them.—**John G. Paton,** SJP, 65

"If God be for us, who can be against us? We may boldly say, The Lord is my helper, and I will not fear what man shall do unto me."

The effect of these words at such a time was remarkable. All realized that God was speaking to us. Never was there a message more directly given to mortal man from his God than that message to us. From almost the first verse my whole soul seemed flooded with a great peace; all trace of panic vanished; and I felt God's presence was with us. Indeed, His presence was so real it could scarcely have been more so had we seen a visible form.—**Rosalind Goforth,** HIK, 54

The Gospel of Jesus Christ is free, but it takes money to keep the Gospel Wagon in Tongaland.—**Malla Moe,** MM, 209

Two distinguishing marks of the early church were: (1) Poverty; (2) Power.—**T.J. Bach,** PMS, 21

One furlough I met a lady who said to me, "I have no interest in anything but my house and my garden. My house and my garden are my life." I thought how pitifully poor she had confessed herself to be; even though hers was a large expensive home and mine a mere shanty on the wild mountainside.—**Isobel Kuhn,** NAA, 166

God's work done in God's way will never lack God's supplies.—**J. Hudson Taylor,** HTS, 120

If the Church stewards . . . were to examine more carefully the integrity and worthwhileness of the institutions to which they are giving their money, as well as the work-ableness of the present methods employed, some so-called Christian projects would pass out of existence along with a good deal of religious racketeering.—**Clarence W. Jones,** RNM, 93

If we are going to wait until every possible hindrance has been removed before we do a work for the Lord, we will never attempt to do anything.—**T.J. Bach,** VFM, 121

The work of the Lord has been put in the hands of His children, and if there is a lack of funds, it must be that they are not doing what they ought to do, what He wants them to do, and what He has told them to do. We are told not to gather treasures here on earth.—**Malla Moe,** MM, 132

We are neither of us inexperienced, unacquainted with the value of money, or unaccustomed either to its want or possession. There are few more cool and calculating, perhaps, than we are; but in all our calculations we calculate on God's faithfulnes, or seek to do so. Hitherto we have not been put to shame, nor have I any anxiety or fear lest we should be in the future.—**J. Hudson Taylor,** EHP, 56

Wants are things we think we need; necessities are things God knows we need. God will supply our needs, not our wants.—**T.J. Bach,** PMS, 41

It must be trust in Him and in Him only, not one little bit in any Society; if they pay our expenses, well and good, but I am not going to trust in God *and* them . . . —**C.T. Studd,** CAP, 125

I get generally so depressed when I am unwell, but now I don't feel in the least cast down. After all these weeks of illness I feel in perfectly good spirits.—**Ion Keith-Falconer,** IKF, 156

Do not think me mad. It is not to make money that I believe a Christian should live. . . . The noblest thing a man can do is, just humbly to receive, and then go amongst others and give.—**David Livingstone,** LAM, 16-17

One cannot help feeling a deep, inward, peaceful consciousness that though we are absolutely shut off from every human help, yet we have protection more secure than any consul can afford, even the omnipotent arm of Jehovah.—**Alexander Mackay,** LAM, 75

Financially, I have almost nothing to show for my 44 years of labor on behalf of the Indians. We own an automobile that you folks gave us two years ago, a home in the jungles of Peru, five hundred dollars in savings for the education of children and that's all. In the wealth of friendship, however, we are millionaires.—**William Cameron Townsend,** UC, 224

I had five children and I never saw a doctor. God did wonderfully.—**Mrs. C.T. Studd,** CAP, 101

We do not tell when we are in need unless definitely asked, and even then not always . . . We rely upon the verses which assure us that our Father knows our needs, and we take it that with such a Father, to know is to supply.—**Amy Carmichael,** CTD, 189

We were counting over our defenses, while waiting in the dugout. Overhead are the overshadowing wings, Psalm 91:4; underneath are the everlasting arms, Deuteronomy 33:27; all around "the angel of the Lord encampeth round about them that fear him, and delivereth them," Psalm 34:7; inside, that "Peace which passeth all understanding," Philippians 4:7; also, "Thou wilt keep him in perfect peace, whose mind is stayed on thee: because he trusteth in thee," Isaiah 26:3.—**Virginia (Mrs. Nelson) Bell,** FDC, 183

From my many years experience I can unhesitatingly say that the cross bears those who bear the cross.—**Sadhu Sundar Singh,** MCC, 49

Many have been the trials and dangers through which we have been called to pass; but hitherto the protecting hand of the Lord has been extended over us and we have been preserved unscathed in the midst of the fire.—**James Stewart Thomas,** BMS, 162

I could not think that God was poor, that He was short of resources, or unwilling to supply any want of whatever work was really His. It seemed to me that if there were lack of funds to carry on work, then to that degree, in that special development, or at that time, it could not be the work of God. To satisfy my conscience I was there compelled to resign my connection with the Society . . . —**J. Hudson Taylor,** HTS, 82

Loneliness

Turn to me and be gracious to me,
for I am lonely and afflicted.
Psalm 25:16

And surely I am with you always,
to the very end of the age.
Matthew 28:20b

I had feelings of fear about the future. . . . The devil kept on whispering, "It's all right now, but what about afterward? You are going to be very lonely." . . . And I turned to my God in a kind of desperation and said, "Lord, what can I do? How can I go on to the end?" And He said, "None of them that trust in Me shall be desolate." That word has been with me ever since.—**Amy Carmichael,** ACD, 62

I mean to be very regular in my writing to you, and very minute, and I shall expect the same at the other end of the line. The danger is that we shall gradually drop out the little details which will make life seem real because they seem so unimportant.—**Luella Miner,** GOG, 60

I pray that no missionary will ever be as lonely as I have been.—**Lottie Moon,** NLM, 275

I have no comfort of any kind but what I have in God. I live in the most lonesome wilderness, and have but one person to converse with that can speak English, an Indian. . . . I have no fellow-Christian to whom I can unbosom myself.—**David Brainerd,** GM, 34-35

All my friends are but One, but He is all sufficient. —**William Carey,** VLM, 15

The ever-merciful Lord sustained me to lay the precious dust of my beloved ones in the same quiet grave . . . and that spot became my sacred and much frequented shrine during all the following months and years when I laboured on for the salvation of these savage Islanders amidst difficulties, dangers and deaths . . . But for Jesus, and the fellowship He vouchsafed me there, I must have gone mad and died beside that lonely grave!—**John G. Paton,** SJP, 36

Jesus is faithful; his promises are precious. Were it not for these considerations, I should, with my present prospects, sink down in despair, especially as no female has, to my knowledge, ever left the shores of America to spend her life among the heathen; nor do I yet know, that I shall have a single female companion. But God is my witness, that I have not dared to decline the offer that has been made me, though so many are ready to call it "a wild, romantic undertaking."—**Ann "Nancy" Judson,** TGS, 86

Shall I tell you what sustained me amidst the toil, the hardship, and loneliness of my exiled life? It was the promise, "Lo, I am with you always, even unto the end."
—**David Livingstone,** LTP, 136

I have never felt homesick since I knew God to be my Father.—**Isabella Thoburn,** LIT, 70

A packet arrived from India without a single letter for me. It was some disappointment to me: but let me be satisfied with my God, and if I cannot have the comfort of hearing from my friends, let me return with thankfulness to His Word ... where I can find what will more than compensate for the loss of earthly enjoyments.—**Henry Martyn,** SAS, 457

For the first time since leaving New York I had to put up a real struggle to drive away the pangs of loneliness and longing. Missionaries are not angels—but ordinary human beings, "subject to like passions as ye all."—**Johanna Veenstra,** JON, 184

There is no one to write and tell all my stories and troubles and nonsense to.—**Mary Slessor,** JIJ, 161

As I wander from village to village, I feel it is no idle fancy that the Master walks beside me and I hear his voice saying gently, "I am with you always, even unto the end."—**Lottie Moon,** NLM, 132

I yesterday received your very welcome letter. It is but the second that I have received, after having written at least two hundred.—**Robert Morrison,** JIJ, 168

The news which he had to tell me, who had been two full years without any tidings from Europe, made my whole frame thrill. The terrible fate that had befallen France, the telegraphic cables successfully laid in the Atlantic, the election of General Grant, the death of good Lord Clarendon, my constant friend; the proof that Her Majesty's Government had not forgotten me in voting a thousand pounds for supplies, and many other points of interest, revived emotions that had been dormant in Manyuema. —**David Livingstone,** LAM, 122-123

How I would love to escape from it all. I find it very hard to endure. . . . For twelve months I have been alone, since there has been no one to send for my help. However, whether alone or with a companion, the Lord is able to work. Sometimes the fewer the workers the greater the work He can do.—**Lilian Hamer,** EHP, 148

Supernatural Power

---

*But you will receive power when the Holy
Spirit comes on you; and you will be my
witnesses in Jerusalem, and in all Judea and
Samaria, and to the ends of the earth.*
Acts 1:8

Whatever else you fail of, do not fail of the influences of
the Holy Spirit; that is the only way you can handle the
consciences of men.—**David Brainerd,** SMP, 18

So many sects, so many opinions, so much want of spirituality, and such shallow talk in the name of religion. All these troubled me very much, and I began to see much the same in the picture of Christianity as I had been accustomed to see in that of the Hindu religion. But all this time I was conscious that God was leading me. I determined not to take the opinion of men as my ground of belief. I went on reading the Bible only, and trusted in God's mercy.—**Pandita Ramabai,** HOC, 18

Have we forgotten that there is a Holy Ghost, that we must insist upon walking upon crutches when we might fly? —**A.J. Gordon,** SMP, 19

It is impossible for us to analyze, dissect or trace by any biological and psychological process the method of this divine mystery. This is all we can distinctly formulate— somewhere down in the depths of our subconscious being God through the Holy Spirit takes up His abode. . . . The Holy Spirit is just as truly in us when He makes no sign as when the fountains of joy are overflowing, or the waters of peace are softly refreshing our weary and troubled hearts.—**A.B. Simpson,** WCC

What we need to be assured of is not that we possess an excellent system of doctrine and ritual, but that the gift of the Holy Ghost is a reality.—**Roland Allen,** MP, 139

Yes, the great Invisible is in the midst of these Karen wilds. That mighty Being, who heaped up these craggy rocks, and reared these stupendous mountains, and poured out these streams in all directions, and scattered immortal beings throughout these deserts—He is present by the influence of his Holy Spirit, and accompanies the sound of the gospel with converting, sanctifying power. The best of all is, God is with us!—**Adoniram Judson,** GM, 297

To my mind the deepest joy of all was to stand still and see the salvation of the Lord. It was not our pleading, it was the touch of God, the divine apart from the human. It was as if veils were suddenly drawn aside, and Gethsemane and Calvary and the Powers of the world to come suddenly became intensely real. . . . The result in our own lives has been, I think, a quickened power of expectation. —**Amy Carmichael,** ACD, 148

We may, indeed, force men to be hypocrites, but no power on earth can force men to become Christians.—**William Carey,** MHM, 57

In these two months I have baptized 289 persons in Mota. It is only a little in one sense; yet to me, knowing the insufficiency of the human agency, it is a proof indeed that the gospel is the power of God unto salvation.—**John Coleridge Patteson,** MCC, 28

And after I had . . . opened to them the glorious remedy provided in Christ for perishing sinners, there was then no vice unreformed, no external duty neglected. The reformation was general, and all springing from the eternal influence of divine truths upon their hearts; not because they had heard these vices particularly exposed and repeatedly spoken against. . . . their eager obedience was not from any rational view of the beauty of morality, but from the internal influence of mercy on the soul.—**David Brainerd,** GM, 40-41

The sense of being led by an unseen hand which takes mine, while another hand reaches ahead and prepares the way, grows upon me daily.—**Frank Laubach,** EOT, 124

We need to know more of the fellowship of Christ's death. We need to feed on the Word of God more than we do. We need more holiness, more prayer. We shall not, then, be in such danger of mistaking his will.—**James O. Fraser,** POF, 20

So to-day the Holy Ghost, if we would but hear His voice, would call a halt on much of our religious activity and even our revival plans and the beckoning finger of the "Man of Macedonia" would call us to the new West which has arisen upon our horizon . . . —**A.B. Simpson,** WCC

It is remarkable that God began this work among the Indians at a time when I had the least hope, and to my apprehension the least rational prospect of success. —**David Brainerd,** JDB, 62-63

I am now in my seventeenth year in China, and I have seen with my own eyes the power of the Gospel of Christ changing the hearts and lives of thousands of people. I see it every day and I know that it works.—**Nelson Bell,** FDC, 145

Take it at its very worst. They are dead lands and dead souls, blind and cold and stiff in death as no heathen are; but we who love them see the possibilities of sacrifice, of endurance, of enthusiasm, of life . . . Does not the Son of God, who died for them, see these possibilities, too? . . . To raise the spiritually dead is the work of the Son of God. —**Lilias Trotter,** ICF, 209

A man or woman, white or black, *must* be full of the Holy
Ghost if he is to stand, and not be lost in sin out here. . . .
We are not out here to please men or to make cheap
reputations for ourselves. We are here to proclaim Christ's
Gospel of repentance, faith, and following Jesus to a finish.
We know of no Gospel, but that of the devil, which does
not demand holiness, downright and practical personal
holiness, as necessary to entrance into heaven.—**C.T.
Studd,** CCF, 100

He has given us a gentle, patient Guide, who is willing to
go with us all the way, and come into the minutest step-
pings of our life.—**A.B. Simpson,** WCC

As soon as we separate quality from the deepest passion
of our Lord to seek and save the lost, it ceases to be
Christian quality. . . . Even if we produce Christians who
live as full brothers with men of other races, but do not
burn with desire that those others may have eternal life,
their "quality" is certainly in doubt.—**Donald McGavran,**
UCG, 52

I do not know how . . . to make a man think seriously about
sin and judgment, and must look to the work of the Holy
Spirit for . . . any hint of such a working.—**Jim Elliot,** SOA, 202

How little chance the Holy Ghost has nowadays. The
churches and missionary societies have so bound Him in
red tape that they practically ask Him to sit in a corner
while they do the work themselves.—**C.T. Studd,** FAF, 120

Character

Love must be sincere.
Hate what is evil; cling to what is good.
Be devoted to one another in brotherly love.
Honor one another above yourselves.
Never be lacking in zeal,
but keep your spiritual fervor,
serving the Lord. Be joyful in hope,
patient in affliction, faithful in prayer.
Romans 12:9-12

So many missionaries, intent on doing something, forget that His main work is to make something of them ... —**Jim Elliot,** SOA, 179

Are you going to do something fine in the New Year? I
trust so. At least you will be good, and To Be is a better
verb than To Do, in my estimation.—**Mary Slessor,** in a
letter to a little girl, HOC, 63

OBEDIENCE to God's will is the secret of spiritual
knowledge and insight. It is not willingness to know, but
willingness to DO (obey) God's Will that brings certainty.
—**Eric Liddell,** TFS, 165

I have always believed that the Good Samaritan went
across the road to the wounded man just because he
wanted to.—**Wilfred Thomason Grenfell,** VLM, 93

The missionary spirit is the spirit of Jesus, the spirit of the
incarnation and the Cross.—**J. Hudson Taylor,** GMC, 109

What Christian worker has not hoped that somehow the
words which he speaks or the books which he distributes
will prove a more effective witness than does his hurried
and ineffective life? But here the missionary commits himself outright to showing Christianity as a way of life, and
this keeps him in constant realization of his need for a
closer walk with God.—**Lyman MacCallum,** CI, 86

The image of the crucified Christ is found much rather in
men who imitate Him in their daily walk than in the
crucifix made of wood.—**Raymond Lull,** RLI, 122

Unless a person is used to thinking himself of considerable
importance, he gets a good deal of a surprise . . . for
important he certainly is in the eyes of the people. . . . It

makes him realize that he, and in so many cases he alone, stands for all those people will know of Jesus Christ. —**Monona Cheney,** GOG, 218

I have great peace of mind, and a firm conviction that I am doing what is right; a feeling that God is directing and ordering the course of my life; and whenever I take the only true view of the business of life I am happy and cheerful.—**John Coleridge Patteson,** BMS, 227

Do not try to limit God to the smallness of your prejudices. God honors many ways of surrendering. Do not try to avoid one method because it hurts your pride.—**Eric Liddell,** DCL, 33

There are many phases to a missionary's life. The least of these is to preach, so you don't have to look for those who are especially gifted or learned to become missionaries. Kindness is the big thing.—**Malla Moe,** MM, 146

Isn't it time that we missionaries part company with those who roll this word *heathen* under their tongues as a sweet morsel of contempt? Shall we Christians at home or in mission fields be courteous in preaching the gladdest tidings on earth, or not? . . . It is time that the followers of Jesus revise their language and learn to speak respectfully of non-Christian peoples.—**Lottie Moon,** NLM, 201

In many cases what God wants is *not* a money contribution, but personal consecration to His service abroad; or the giving up of a son or a daughter—more precious than silver or gold—to His service. . . . no amount of money can convert a single soul. What is needed is that men and women filled with the Holy Ghost should give *themselves* to the work.—**J. Hudson Taylor,** JHT, 177

There is nothing like work on the mission field for widening one's horizon. Where I am exactly I don't know, . . . I know John iii.16, and that's good enough holding ground for my anchor. When I see the littleness of some of you Christians I am glad to be away from it all, . . . Our Christianity is too much a matter of words, and far too little a matter of works. One might think that works were of the devil by the assiduity with which the great proportion of our church members keep clear of them.—**George Grenfell,** PIC, 147

The power of educated womanhood is simply the power of skilled service. We are not in the world to be ministered unto, but to minister. The world is full of need, and every opportunity to help is a duty.—**Isabella Thoburn,** SOK, 138

. . . The heart of Christ is not only the heart of a man but has in it also all the tenderness and gentleness of woman.—**A.B. Simpson,** WCC

. . . undoubtedly the most permanent contributions conferred on the coast by the many college students, who come as volunteers every summer to help us in the various branches of our work, is just this gift of their own personalities.—**Wilfred Thomason Grenfell,** ALD, 185

I here wish to emphasize that we live amongst the natives in no sense as chiefs, or masters . . . if we begin to give ourselves airs, the native Christians would not be with us at all.—**William Johnson,** JNN, 106

To have the best furniture, to set the best table, to dress better than one's neighbors are motives which tempt many a mind that ought to be too strong for attack. . . . All this self-seeking is a weary, dreary effort, which either results in loss and disappointment that makes the heart sick, or in success, which is the dreariest thing of all, and most to be regretted. When we seek for dross thinking it gold, empty-handed failure is better than to come into possession of that which is worthless, while it wears a form of use and beauty.—**Isabella Thoburn,** LIT, 240

If we could only remember that God has always gloried in choosing the foolish things, the weak things, the base things and the things which are not in order that His power might be revealed to us in our weakness and through us that the glory might be all His.—**Kenneth Strachan,** WSA, 142

Do not be sensitive. Perhaps you are by nature, but you can get over it with the exercise of common sense and the help of God. Let things hurt until the tender spot gets callous. Believe that people do not intend to be unkind; some are too busy to think of the feelings of their fellow-workers, and others have not the nice discernment that ought to guide even the busy brain and tongue. Sensitive-ness is only another kind of self-consciousness, and as such we should seek deliverance from its irritating power. —**Isabella Thoburn,** LIT, 258

Warfare—Within and Without

The great dragon was hurled down—that
ancient serpent called the devil, or Satan, who
leads the whole world astray. He was hurled to
the earth, and his angels with him.
They overcame him by the blood of the Lamb
and by the word of their testimony;
they did not love their lives so much
as to shrink from death.
Revelation 12:9, 11

The only person who does not believe that the Devil is a person is someone who has never attempted to combat him or his ways. . . . The simple tribesman going through his animistic incantations is wiser than such a drugged intellectual. He, at least, knows there is a Devil; and he has ways to appease him temporarily.—**Isobel Kuhn,** ATT, 197-198

Infighting among personnel is more devilish, desperate, and devastating than anything from the outside.—**Clarence W. Jones,** CUM, 37

I have ever found it, when I have thought the battle was over and the conquest gained, and so let down my watch, the enemy has risen up and done me the greatest injury. —**David Brainerd,** TWP, 32

. . . the feeling among us appears to have been worse than I could have formed any conception of. One was jealous because another had too many new dresses, another because someone else had more attention. Some were wounded because of unkind controversial discussions, and so on. Thank God for bringing it out and removing it.—**J. Hudson Taylor,** HTM, 147

On Saturday we drove to the station, found all the ladies in tears, and their husbands pale and trembling. We all consulted together what was best to be done; but what else could we do? Every place seemed as unsafe as this. . . . We came home, the four families to our house, and spent the day in conversation and prayer, expecting every moment to hear the shout of the infuriated mob; the day, however, passed quietly. At night, our husbands took turns to watch in front of the Bungalows.—**Elizabeth Freeman,** MFM, 189

Tension does some good things. A reasonable number of fleas is good for a dog. It keeps him from brooding over being a dog.—**Clarence W. Jones,** YHI, 39

It was with shocking suddenness that I realized the work of an enemy among us; an oppressing atmosphere of criticism had suddenly developed among our little well-beloved group of workers, and I saw no human causes for it . . . We confessed our faults and sins to one another and to God. . . . Tears mingled, and tension broke; the winds of God swept throughout our household . . . We knew now that there was nothing to hinder God's blessing to us on behalf of others.—**Joy Ridderhof,** MS, 35-36

The great causes of God and humanity are not defeated by the hot assaults of the Devil, but by the slow, crushing, glacier-like mass of thousands and thousands of indifferent nobodies. God's causes are never destroyed by being blown up, but by being sat upon.—George Adam Smith, as quoted by **Wilfred Thomason Grenfell,** ALD, 299

I cannot tell you how I am buffeted sometimes by temptation. I never knew how bad a heart I have. Yet I do know that I love God and love His work, and desire to serve Him only and in all things. And I value above all else that precious Saviour in whom alone I can be accepted.—**J. Hudson Taylor,** HTS, 153

When [a government policy] is found to be one which . . . concerns the souls fully as much as the bodies of men, affecting the interests of eternity not less than those of time—the Christian missionary must not, dares not, be silent, even if his voice should be uplifted against kings and governors and all earthly potentates.—**Alexander Duff,** in a letter to Governor-General Lord Auckland, RAD, 151

Of slave mothers and strangled widows, of burnings, mutilations, witchcraft, of hideous cruelties and brutish outrage that make up the picture of women's life in Africa and the dark islands of the sea, it is impossible to write without seeming wilfully to exaggerate horrors.—**Helen Barrett Montgomery,** WWE, 52

I have just finished translating the Ten Commandments. "They are very good," the people say; but none is willing to be fettered by the awkward conditions involved by accepting them. They would be very glad if their neighbours would accept them, for they can see the advantage of living among well-behaved people. They cannot at all see, though, why a Supreme Being should trouble about their dealings one with the other, and why they should be answerable to Him for their wrongdoings.—**George Grenfell,** PIC, 139

China is open to all; but my time and strength are too short, and the work too great to allow of my attempting to work with any who do not agree with me in the main on my plans of action . . . —**J. Hudson Taylor,** JHT, 211

Do pray for our real union in heart; I think it is very difficult for some to realize our union in life and soul, amidst such differences of disposition.—**William Johnson,** JNN, 151

When in hand-to-hand conflict with the world and the devil, neat little biblical confectionery is like shooting lions with a pea-shooter: one needs a man who will let himself go and deliver blows right and left as hard as he can hit, trusting in the Holy Ghost.—**C.T. Studd,** CAP, 167

There are two or three circumstances in the Mission which occasion us pain; I mean the un-missionary spirit which operates in a love of ease, an anxiety for European society, and other things of the same nature which enervate the soul of a missionary and unfit him for his work.—**William Carey,** WCM, 295

View your pressures no longer as burdens but as a platform for His glorious sufficiency.—**Clarence W. Jones,** YHI, 39

Outside a certain temple a little man . . . ran hither and thither . . . trying to chase the people away . . . Then he sent an ugly old fellow to beat a drum right in front of us. We sang on just the same . . . It worked out for good; he gathered a big crowd. But now, what happened? A policeman came out and stopped the noise; the little man flew like a cat into his corner, and we got a lovely chance to speak to the amazed crowd.—a woman in one of **Pandita Ramabai's** Gospel Bands, PR, 119

I hear someone coming up the hill in my direction. He is afraid because of the demons and the darkness, so as he climbs he chants to them. . . . demon power enslav[es] the people until they are ruled by fear. Yet as this lamp on my table by its light dispels the shadows, so God has given to me this glorious light of the gospel to shine out to all around.—**Lilian Hamer,** EHP, 144

In South India a great caste—the Ezhavas—decided to become Christians. . . . After the decision a lawyer arose and said: "Now you have decided to be Christians. What kind of Christians will you be—Church of England, Baptist, or some other denomination? Now you are united as a caste. In the future you will be divided as these denominations are." They never became Christians. That killed it.—**E. Stanley Jones,** CWM, 267

It doesn't matter, really, how great the pressure is; it only matters *where the pressure lies*. See that it never comes *between* you and the Lord—then, the greater the pressure, the more it presses you to His breast.—**J. Hudson Taylor,** HTS, 152

The devil does not care how many hospitals we build . . . if only he can pull our ideals down, and sidetrack us. —**Amy Carmichael,** CTD, 291

God is already using this withdrawal of the missionaries and this persecution of the Church in China . . . He is only going to permit the trials and persecutions to go far enough to purify the Church.—**Nelson Bell,** FDC, 98

Pre-pray your pressure points.—**Clarence W. Jones,** YHI, 47

There is the constant invisible warfare that has to be waged against the powers of darkness. . . . It is fashionable in the Western world to relegate belief in demons and devils to the realm of mythology, and when mentioned at all it is a matter of jest. But it is no jest in West Africa or any other mission field for that matter.—**Rowland Bingham,** JIJ, 297

The missionaries in the interior are, I am grieved to say, a sorry set. . . . I shall be glad when I get away . . . from their envy and back-biting.—**David Livingstone,** JIJ, 148

Oh! how well doth it make for peace to be silent about others, not to believe everything without discernment, and not to go on easily telling things.—**Robert E. Speer,** MSG, 171

Let us not return evil for evil, the long expected day has come, and the time of our departure is at hand. Strengthen yourselves in the Lord, and He will redeem your souls. Be not afraid of those who can only kill the body, but put your trust in God, Who will speedily give you His eternal reward, and an entrance into His heavenly kingdom. —**Boniface,** before his martyrdom, BMS, 43

The governor, General Murray, will not allow me to teach any of the slaves to read; but I find quite enough to do to teach the poor free children and adults. . . . While we see the cause of God prosper on the one hand, on the other we are violently opposed by a multitude of enemies.—**John Smith,** BMS, 86

Envied by some, despised by many, hated by others, often blamed for things I never heard of or had nothing to do with, an innovator on what have become established rules of missionary practice, an opponent of mighty systems of heathen error and superstition, working without precedent in many respects and with few experienced helpers, often sick in body as well as perplexed in mind and embarrassed by circumstances—had not the Lord been specially gracious to me, had not my mind been sustained by the conviction that the work is His and that He is with me in what it is no empty figure to call "the thick of the conflict," I must have fainted or broken down. But the battle *is* the Lord's, and He will conquer. We may fail—do fail continually—but He never fails. Still, I need your prayers more than ever.—**J. Hudson Taylor,** HTS, 152

To this work you have pledged yourselves by solemn vow and promise and I see you now, waiting with impatience to enter the field of battle—your weapons, deeds of charity; your shield, gentleness and patience; your teaching, that of example; your triumph, the heroic sacrifice of your life.—**Charles Lavigerie,** ATA, 132

Faith

*By faith Abraham, when called to go to a place
he would later receive as his inheritance,
obeyed and went, even though he did not know
where he was going. By faith he made his
home in the promised land like a stranger in a
foreign country; he lived in tents, as did
Isaac and Jacob, who were heirs with him
of the same promise. For he was looking
forward to the city with foundations
whose architect and builder is God.*
Hebrews 11:8-10

If God had suddenly shown us everything he was going to do in the years to come, I would have said, "Wait a minute, you've got the wrong man! . . ." But God inched up the curtain just a little bit at a time and said, "Take a look, and take a step."—**Clarence W. Jones,** CUM, 82

During those early pioneer years, when laying the foundation of the Changte Church, my own weak faith was often rebuked when I saw the results of the simple, childlike faith of our Chinese Christians. Some of those answers to prayer were of such an extraordinary character that, when told in the homeland, even ministers expressed doubts as to their genuineness.—**Rosalind Goforth,** HIK, 42-43

It seems as though the Lord had chosen the most unpromising places in which to reveal Himself in might and power, and to encourage us to go forward.—**George Grenfell,** PIC, 126

True faith glories in the present tense, and does not trouble itself about the future. God's promises are in the present tense, and are quite secure enough to set our hearts at rest. Their full outworking is often in the future, but God's word is as good as His bond and we need have no anxiety.—**James O. Fraser,** POF, 9

It is a tragedy when a man has no invisible means of support.—**T.J. Bach,** PMS, 41

My readers may think me an optimist, but a Christian has no right to be anything else. This is God's world, not the devil's. It is ruled by one who is "the Lord our Righteousness," "the same yesterday and to-day, yea, and for ever."—**Henry Benjamin Whipple,** SOK, 32

The use of means ought not to lessen our faith in God, and our faith in God ought not to hinder our using whatever means he has given us for the accomplishment of his own purposes.—**J. Hudson Taylor,** SOM, 166

Friends are saying to me, "What are people who are living by faith going to do when money gets tight and depression comes?" The thought came to me that the real question is, "What are people who are not living by faith going to do?"—**Joy Ridderhof,** PMS, 41

The eagle that soars in the upper air does not worry itself how it is to cross rivers.—**Gladys Aylward,** TW, 167

I am going to a new tribe up-country, a fierce, cruel people, and every one tells me they will kill me. But I don't fear any hurt. Only—to combat their savage customs will require courage and firmness on my part.—**Mary Slessor,** WQO, 51

Give me faith to take courage, in the midst of apparent discouragements, to confide in Thy promise, even when all things seem to be against me.—**Allen Gardiner,** CAG, 35

It has been my lot in life to have to stand by many deathbeds, and to be called in to dying men and women almost as a routine in my profession. Yet I am increasingly convinced that their spirits never die at all. I am sure that there is no real death. Death is no argument against, but rather for, life. Eternal life is the complement of all my unsatisfied ideals; and experience teaches me that the belief in it is a greater incentive to be useful and good than any other I know.—**Wilfred Thomason Grenfell,** ALD, 300

There are two little words in our language which I always admired—TRY and TRUST. You know not what you can or cannot effect until you try; and if you make your trials in the exercise of trust in God, mountains of imaginary difficulties will vanish as you approach them, and facilities will arise which you never anticipated.—**John Williams,** GM, 75

The more obstacles you have, the more opportunities there are for God to do something.—**Clarence W. Jones,** CUM, 61

Expect great things from God. Attempt great things for God.—**William Carey,** GM, 220

I love to live on the brink of eternity.—**David Brainerd,** HOF, 27

How often do we attempt work for God to the limit of our incompetency rather than to the limit of God's omnipotency.—**J. Hudson Taylor,** CMM, 129

God will work out big things from the War, for there is no waste with Him.—**Mary Slessor,** WQO, 200

I like men whose vision carries them far beyond their own horizons.—**Kenneth Strachan,** WSA, 98-99

It is not unnatural that man, realizing that he is himself like "the grass that to-morrow is cast into the oven," should worry over the permanency of the things on which he had spent himself. Though Christ especially warns us against this anxiety, religious people have been the greatest sin-

ners in laying more emphasis on to-morrow than to-day.
—**Wilfred Thomason Grenfell,** ALD, 295

"If this is a war," the message said, "A woman is not likely
to stop it." Back went her reply. "You think only of the
woman. You have forgotten the woman's God."—quoting
Mary Slessor, WQO, 79

God's part is to put forth His power; our part is to put forth
faith.—**Andrew A. Bonar,** TWP, 119

All the resources of the Godhead are at our disposal!
—**Jonathan Goforth,** CMM, 197

Future missionaries will be rewarded by conversions for
every sermon. . . . Let them not forget . . . us, who worked
when all was gloom, and no evidence of success in the way
of conversion cheered our paths.—**David Livingstone,**
DL, 41

. . . I never prayed sincerely or earnestly for anything, but
it came. At some time, no matter how distant a day, somehow, in some shape, probably the last I should have
devised, it came. And yet I have always had so little faith.
May God forgive me . . . and cleanse the sin of unbelief
from my heart.—**J. Hudson Taylor,** GMC, 111

I belong to the Church and she has plenty of time.
—**Charles de Foucauld,** ATA, 339

When God's finger points, God's hand will open the
door.—**Clarence W. Jones,** CUM, 65

My greatest experience on the mission field is meeting impossible circumstances with Someone who makes them possible. It is the deep thrill that comes from facing something you know you can't do—and finding your weakness suddenly turned into strength. That's something exciting.—**Carl K. Becker,** AHM, 128

This was many times a comfort to me, that life and death did not depend upon my choice; I was pleased to think that He who is infinitely wise, had the determination of this matter . . . I had little strength to pray, none to write or read, and scarce any to meditate; but, through divine goodness, I could with great composure look death in the face, and frequently with sensible joy. O how blessed it is to be habitually prepared for death!—**David Brainerd,** LDB, 148

But how to get faith strengthened? Not by striving after faith, but by resting on the Faithful One.—**J. Hudson Taylor,** quoting his friend, McCarthy, HTS, 161

Philosophy of Ministry

*For the earth will be filled
with the knowledge of the glory of the LORD,
as the waters cover the sea.*
Habakkuk 2:14

*So whether you eat or drink or whatever you
do, do it all for the glory of God. Do not cause
anyone to stumble, whether Jews, Greeks or
the church of God—even as I try to please
everybody in every way. For I am not seeking
my own good but the good of many, so that
they may be saved. Follow my example,
as I follow the example of Christ.*
1 Corinthians 10:31—11:1

Rome was not built in a day, nor will the work of building up a strong, well-instructed body of Lisu Christians in the Tengyueh district be the work of a day either. . . . God has brought me to the point of being willing for it to be in His time as well as in His way. I am even willing . . . not to see the fullness of blessing in my life-time.—**James O. Fraser,**
MR, 102

We dare not go on awakening interest in the Gospel unless somehow we can nourish and preserve the results. —**Clarence W. Jones,** CTV, 89

The kingdom of God is a new order founded on the fatherly love of God, on redemption, justice, and fellowship. It is meant to enter into all life, all nations, and all policies till the kingdoms of this world become the kingdom of our Lord.—**Eric Liddell,** DCL, 83

My denominational affiliation is found in Psalm 119:63: "I am a companion of all them that fear Thee, and of them that keep Thy precepts."—**T.J. Bach,** PMS, 37

[The Indian] is making an amazing . . . discovery, namely that Christianity and Jesus are not the same—that they may have Jesus without the system that has been built up around him in the West.—**E. Stanley Jones,** COR, 23

An earthly organization does not become the church; it corrupts her.—**Roland Allen,** ROM, 209

The comparative study of religion may broaden our minds and give us new points of contact with non-Christians; but the study of positive religion revealed in the mind and life of Christ will fill us with a missionary passion for God's glory. Again, this motive tests all of our methods. —**Samuel M. Zwemer,** TMW, 69

Why should a foreign aspect be given to Christianity? We wish to see churches of such believers presided over by pastors and officers of their own countrymen, worshipping God in their own tongue, in edifices of a thoroughly native style.—**J. Hudson Taylor,** VLM, 44

Where the geographical feat ends, there the missionary work begins.—**David Livingstone,** MHM, 292

We must resist the temptation to grab some of the glory for the organization we are promoting. Our deputation messages, our prayer letters, our promotional literature must all be characterized by the presence of that which glorifies God.—**Kenneth Strachan,** WSA, 91

Here opens upon us the glimpse of a dreadful crisis. Give them knowledge without religion, according to the present Government plan, and they will become *a nation of infidels!*—**Alexander Duff,** RAD, 99

Civilization is not necessary before Christianity; do both together if you will, but you will find civilization follow Christianity more easily than Christianity follow civilization.—**Samuel Marsden,** MHM, 125

I have never been in any sense what is generally understood by the term "faith healer," but I am certain that you can make a new man out of an old one, can save a man who is losing ground, and turn the balance and help him to win out through psychic agencies when all our chemical stimulants are only doing harm.—**Wilfred Thomason Grenfell,** ALD, 275

We are, as it were, God's agents—used by Him to do His work, not ours. We do our part, and then can only look

to Him, with others, for His blessing.—**James O. Fraser,**
POF, 8

The things that really count are the things we cannot
count.—**T.J. Bach,** PMS, 41

The world needs Christ more than it needs skills. It will
not accept Christ unless we offer it help with these other
things. But if we give skill without character, we make the
world only more powerful to do itself harm.—**Frank
Laubach,** EOT, 155

There is a real relation between Christian missions and
social progress but to confound the two or make them
co-ordinate is fatal.—**Samuel M. Zwemer,** TMW, 62

As the Law to the Jews, so Islam to the Arabs, is a schoolmaster to bring them to Christ.—**Ion Keith-Falconer,** IKF, 110

No lie is so dangerous as a half-truth and so here we need
the greatest circumspection if we are to teach men to bring
their family life to God; we must be true Englishmen and
loyal subjects but this must not dim the reality of our tribe
the Church, and our Lord the Christ.—**William Johnson,**
JNN, 132-133

Christianity should teach men how to be saved for eternity,
but also how to live comfortably and healthily together.
—**David Livingstone,** LAM, 17

In the discharge of our ministry we will not knowingly link
ourselves to anyone who denies our Lord. At the same

time, in faithfulness to Scriptural injunction and example, we shall not necessarily cut ourselves off from contacts which might result in the correction of an erring brother or the salvation of some captive soul.—**Kenneth Strachan,** WSA, 144

One can't save and then pitchfork souls into heaven . . . Souls are more or less securely fastened to bodies . . . and as you can't get the souls out and deal with them separately, you have to take them both together.—**Amy Carmichael,** CTD, 247

No people ever rise higher, as a people, than the point to which they elevate their women.—**Isabella Thoburn,** LIT, 78

We have a whole Christ for our salvation; a whole Bible for our staff; a whole Church for our fellowship; and a whole world for our parish.—**John Chrysostom,** ITG, 68

I would rather have one thoroughly trained and tested and efficient Nez Perce minister and pastor, than half a dozen half taught and half tested.—**Sue McBeth,** GGC, 92

It is Christ who has made woman free and equal. Is she to be allowed this freedom and equality elsewhere and denied it in the Church, where freedom and equality had their origin? The Christian Churches on the foreign mission field are apprehending the measure of the Gospel in this better than we. . . . God shuts no doors to His daughters which He opens to His sons.—**Robert E. Speer,** MSG, 163

I am satisfied that unless one's whole heart and life form the key to the understanding of the mystery of sin, the case of the sinner, and the power of the Gospel, our preaching cannot be effective, and knowledge of the Bible will be little more than intellectual.—**John Coleridge Patteson,** BMS, 224

We do good to others, not in the measure of our words or actions, but in the measure of what we are . . . He who would be useful to souls must first labor with all his strength and continuously at the task of achieving his own personal sanctification.—**Charles de Foucauld,** ATA 340

Sacrifice and Reward

For it has been granted to you
on behalf of Christ not only to believe on him,
but also to suffer for him, since you are going
through the same struggle you saw I had,
and now hear that I still have.
Philippians 1:29-30

When He asks for and receives our all, He gives in return that which is above price—His own presence. The price is not great when compared with what He gives in return; it is our blindness and our unwillingness to yield that make it seem great.—**Rosalind Goforth,** HIK, 68

If God has made it our duty to leave our home and friends, he has given us a home here in the land of strangers . . . If he has presented dark and gloomy prospects . . . yet he has enabled us to trust him in the dark, to feel our entire dependence on him . . .—**Ann "Nancy" Judson,** MMJ, 62

I have written and printed a second edition of the Bengali grammar, and collected materials for a Mahratta dictionary. Besides this, I preach twice a week, frequently thrice, and attend upon my collegiate duties. I do not mention this because I think my work a burden—it is a real pleasure—but to show that my not writing many letters is not because I neglect my brethren, or wish them to cease writing to me.—**Henry Martyn,** MHM, 47

Did you think the missionary path was all glory? Then you have never read of God's greatest Messenger to earth, who sat and wept over Jerusalem, crying out, "I would . . . but ye would not."—**Isobel Kuhn,** ATT, 172

My understanding leaves me, my memory fails me, my utterance fails me; but, *I thank God, my charity holds out still.* I find *that* rather grows than fails.—**John Eliot,** GM, 29

When we arrived in 1937 there were no doctors, no hospitals, no drugstores, no preachers, no communication, no telephones, no aeroplanes. There was just one boat every ten days, weather permitting. But there were 900 Indians and 1100 others, mostly miners and fishermen, in our area. We needed tools to serve these souls and God gave them to us. But first He gave us a burden, then the people, then the means.—a Dr. McClean, MHV, 77

As respects our temporal privations, use has made them familiar and easy to be born; they are of short duration, and when brought in competition with the worth of human souls, sink into nothing.—**Ann "Nancy" Judson,** MMJ, 112

With thee, O my God, is no disappointment. I shall never have to regret that I have loved thee too well.—**Henry Martyn,** GM, 256

Winter travelling on this coast oftentimes involves considerable hardships, as when once our doctor lost the track and he and his men had to spend several nights in the woods. They were so reduced by hunger that they were obligated to chew pieces of green sealskin which they cut from their boots and to broil their skin gloves over a fire which they had kindled.—**Wilfred Thomason Grenfell,** ALD, 143

Circumstances may appear to wreck our lives and God's plans, but *God is not helpless among the ruins.* Our broken lives are not lost or useless. God's love is still working. He comes in and takes the calamity and uses it victoriously, working out his wonderful plan of love.—**Eric Liddell,** DCL, 125

Little did I think, when I last wrote, that I should so soon . . . communicate that one Burman has embraced the Christian religion, and given good evidence of being a true disciple. . . . This event, this single trophy of victorious grace, has filled our hearts with sensations, hardly to be conceived by Christians in Christian countries.—**Ann "Nancy" Judson,** MMJ, 152

In the earthly life of the Christian there may be promotions but there is only one graduation—and that is to Heaven!
—**T.J. Bach,** VFM, 66

In September 1944, as my husband, baby son and I left for our furlough, we had to come out over that high trail; and as we came to the one little mound under the pine tree, I stopped to look back, and say goodbye to Lisuland. . . . everywhere I looked . . . I could see little villages clinging to ridge or shoulder, little "nests" above the abysmal ravines, nests that I knew were now Christian. We were leaving a church roll of some twelve hundred.—**Isobel Kuhn,** NAA, 39

These past fifteen years I have visited fifteen provinces, held 183 missions, and those going through the enquiry rooms showing their desire of wanting to follow Jesus Christ have been 5,342 women and girls.—**Jessie Gregg,** EHP, 82

Thus died a man who had been a cannibal chief, but by the grace of God and the love of Jesus changed, transfigured into a character of light and beauty. I lost, in losing him, one of my best friends and most courageous helpers; but I . . . know . . . there is one soul at least from Tanna to sing the glories of Jesus in Heaven—and oh, the rapture when I meet him there!—**John G. Paton,** SJP, 81

I can assure you that months and months of heart-rending anguish are before you, whether you will or not. Yet take the bitter cup with both hands, and sit down to your repast. You will soon learn a secret, that there is sweetness at the bottom. . . .—**Adoniram Judson,** TGS, 400-401

When we only seek eminence and position, how few avenues are open! When we seek service, how many—all with wide gates, and loud calls, and pleading invitations, to come where work, and room, and reward await all! —**Isabella Thoburn,** LIT, 246

Do not always look for gratitude, for, sometimes when you are most deserving, you will get the least. Do not expect too much of your patients, do not betray surprise or be aggravated if you find they are taking medicine from half a dozen other doctors.—**Ida Scudder,** address to medical school graduates, DII, 165

The pioneer missionary, in overcoming obstacles and difficulties, has the privilege not only of knowing Christ and the power of His resurrection, but also something of the fellowship of His suffering.—**Samuel Zwemer,** STV, 122

What we give up for Christ we gain. What we keep back for ourselves is our real loss.—**J. Hudson Taylor,** CML, 246

Today it is thirteen years ago since I first set foot on African soil. As one looks back over the varying experiences, some of them mountain peaks of joy, and others valleys of depression and disappointments, one is led to humble gratitude to Him who all the way leadeth His children. My heart is full of joy at the remembrance of all His love. —**Johanna Veenstra,** JON, 195

In all my trials and labors for souls, my comfort, my hope, my inspiration was the cross of Christ. Since for me Christ forsook heaven and took upon Himself the burden of the cross, it is no great matter that I have taken up my cross to gain souls *for Him*.—**Sadhu Sundar Singh,** MCC, 47

Dr. Duff, one of the great educators, said, "You might as well try to scale a wall fifty feet high as to educate the women of India." The wall has not only been scaled, but thrown down. The women have been reached and taught, and now they wait for the advantages and opportunities their brothers have received without asking.—**Isabella Thoburn,** LIT, 325

Permit us to labor on in obscurity, and at the end of twenty years you may hear from us again.—**Adoniram Judson,** to the churches back home, GM, 289

For three years we had toiled and prayed and taught for this. At the moment when I put the bread and wine into those dark hands, once stained with the blood of cannibalism, but now stretched out to receive and partake the emblems and seals of the Redeemer's love, I had a foretaste of the joy of Glory that well-nigh broke my heart to pieces. I shall never taste a deeper bliss till I gaze on the glorified face of Jesus Himself.—**John G. Paton,** SJP, 180

I never made a sacrifice. Of this we ought not to talk when we remember the great sacrifice which *He* made who left His Father's throne on high to give Himself for us.—**David Livingstone,** DL, 57

Walked twenty miles with no socks, feet sore and shoes worn to pieces. . . . for the last two days, if I stopped for a minute to drink a coconut, my legs were so stiff they did not get into play for five minutes or so.—**John Coleridge Patteson,** MCC, 20

Without a doubt there comes to many of us the choice between a life of contraction and one of expansion; a life of small dimensions and one of widening horizons and larger visions and plans; a life of self-satisfaction or self-seeking and one of unselfish or truly Christ-like sharing. —**John R. Mott,** ITG, 177

There has never been a single regret that I left the "bright lights and gay life" of New York City, and came to this very dark corner of his vineyard. There has been no sacrifice, because the Lord Jesus Himself is my constant companion.—**Johanna Veenstra,** JON, 129

There is no death. It is all life; only life; eternal life. —**Isabella Thoburn,** LIT, 343

I thank God that I can say my duty is my delight, and the encouraging proofs I have that I do not labour in vain or spend my strength for nought encourages me to "Labour on at God's command, and offer all my works to Him." —**John Whitely,** BMS, 224

Christ's presence has turned my prison into a blessed heaven. What then will His presence do for me in heaven hereafter?—**Sadhu Sundar Singh,** while in prison, MCC, 54

Biographical Information

Allen, Roland, 1868-1947, China

Aylward, Gladys, 1902-1970, China

Bach, T.J. (Thomas John), 1881-1963, Venezuela

Baker, Thomas, 1822-1867, Fiji

Becker, Carl K., 1884-1990, Congo

Bell, Nelson, 1894-1973, China

Bell, Virginia, n.d., China

Bingham, Rowland, 1872-1942, Nigeria

Bonar, Andrew A., 1810-1892, Palestine

Boniface, 680-754, Thuringia and Bavaria

Brainerd, David, 1718-1747, North American Indians

Brewster, Tom, 1939-1985, language consultant

Carey, William, 1761-1834, India

Carmichael, Amy, 1867-1951, India

Chalmers, James, 1841-1901, Polynesia, New Guinea

Cheney, Monona, early 1900s, China

Chestnut, Eleanor, d. 1905, China

Chrysostom, John, c. 344/354-407, Bishop of Constantinople

de Foucauld, Charles, 1858-1916, North Africa

Deyneka, Peter, 1898-1987, founder of Slavic Gospel
    Association

Duff, Alexander, 1806-1878, India

Edman, V. Raymond, 1900-1967, Ecuador

Eliot, John, 1604-1690, North American Indians and Negro
    slaves

Elliot, Jim, 1927-1956, Ecuador

Franson, Frederik, 1852-1908, Scandinavia and Germany

Fraser, James O., 1886-1938, China

Freeman, Elizabeth, d. 1858, India

Gardiner, Allen, 1794-1851, South America

Goforth, Jonathan, 1859-1936, China

Goforth, Rosalind, 1864-1942, China

Gordon, Adoniram Judson, 1836-1895, founded school for training missionaries (now Gordon College)

Gregg, Jessie, early 1900s, China

Grenfell, George, 1849-1906, Congo

Grenfell, Wilfred Thomason, 1865-1940, Iceland and Labrador

Hamer, Lilian, 1910-1958, Thailand

Johnson, William, 1854-1928, West Africa

Jones, Clarence W., 1900-1986, Ecuador

Jones, E. Stanley, 1884-1973, India

Judson, Adoniram, 1788-1850, Burma

Judson, Ann "Nancy," 1789-1826, Burma

Keith-Falconer, Ion, 1856-1887, Arabian Peninsula

Kuhn, Isobel, 1901-1957, China

Larson, Reuben, 1897-1981, Ecuador

Laubach, Frank, 1884-1970, linguist in Asia, Africa, and Latin America

Lavigerie, Charles, 1825-1892, Africa

Liddell, Eric, 1902-1945, China

Livingstone, David, 1813-1873, Africa

Lull, Raymond, 1232-1316, Tunis, Algeria

M'Cheyne, Robert Murray, 1813-1843, Scottish minister, Palestine, Europe

MacCallum, Lyman, n.d., Turkey

Mackay, Alexander, 1849-1890, Uganda

Marsden, Samuel, 1764-1838, New Zealand, Australia

Martyn, Henry, 1781-1812, India, Persia

McBeth, Sue, 183?-1893, North American Indians

McClure, Don, 1906-1977, Ethiopia

McGavran, Donald, 1897-1990, India

Miner, Luella, early 1900s, China

Moe, Petra Malena "Malla," 1863-1953, South Africa

Moffat, Mary, 1795-1871, South Africa

Moffat, Robert, 1795-1883, South Africa

Montgomery, Helen Barrett, 1861-deceased, missionary stateswoman

Moon, Charlotte "Lottie," 1840-1912, China

Morrison, Robert, 1782-1834, China

Mott, John R., 1865-1955, chairman of Student Volunteer Movement for Foreign Missions

Paton, John G., 1824-1907, New Hebrides

Patteson, John Coleridge, 1827-1871, Melanesia

Polycarp, Saint, 70-155/160, Bishop of Smyrna

Ramabai, Pandita, 1858-1922, India

Ridderhof, Joy, d. 1984, Gospel Recordings

Saint, Nate, 1923-1956, Ecuador

Savage, Robert, 1914-1987, Ecuador

Scudder, Ida, 1870-1960, India

Simpson, A.B., 1843-1919, founder of Christian and Missionary Alliance

Singh, Sadhu Sundar, 1889-1929, India, Tibet

Slessor, Mary, 1848-1915, Calabar, Nigeria

Smith, John, 1790-1824, Demerara, British Guiana

Smith, Mrs. John, n.d., Demerara, British Guiana

Somervell, Howard, 1890-1975, India

Speer, Robert E., 1867-1947, secretary, Presbyterian Board of Foreign Missions

Stam, Elizabeth "Betty," 1906-1934, China

Stam, John, 1907-1934, China

Strachan, Kenneth, 1910-1965, Costa Rica

Studd, C.T., 1860-1931, Central Africa

Studd, Mrs. C.T., n.d., Central Africa

Swain, Clara, 1834-1910, India

Sydenstricker, Carie, n.d. available, China

Taylor, J. Hudson, 1832-1905, China

Taylor, Maria, 1837-1870, China

Thoburn, Isabella, 1840-1901, India

Thomas, James Stewart, d. 1856, South Africa

Thompson, Henry Paget, 1880-n.d., India

Threlfall, William, 1799-1826, South Africa

Townsend, William Cameron, 1896-1982, Peru, Mexico

Trotter, Lilias, 1853-1928, North Africa

Tucker, Charlotte, 1821-1893, India

Veenstra, Johanna, 1894-1933, Nigeria

Whipple, Henry Benjamin, no information available

Whitely, John, 1806-1869, New Zealand

Williams, John, 1796-1839, Polynesia

Zinzendorf, Nicholaus Ludwig, 1700-1769, founder of Moravian Church

Zwemer, Samuel, 1867-1952, Arabian Peninsula

Bibliography

(alphabetical by title)

Adventure in Africa, by Charles Partee. Grand Rapids: Ministry Resources Library (Zondervan), 1990.

African Heroes and Heroines, by H.K.W. Kumm. New York: The MacMillan Company, 1917.

Africa's Twelve Apostles. Boston: Daughters of St. Paul, 1981.

Amy Carmichael of Dohnavur: The Story of a Lover and her Beloved, by Frank Houghton. London: S.P.C.A., 1953.

Another Hand on Mine: The Story of Dr. Carl K. Becker of the Africa Inland Mission, by William J. Petersen. New York: McGraw-Hill Book Company, 1967.

Ascent to the Tribes: Pioneering in North Thailand, by Isobel Kuhn. London: China Inland Mission (Lutterworth Press), 1956.

At Your Orders, Lord! by Robert Savage. Grand Rapids: Zondervan, 1957.

The Bridges of God, by Donald McGavran. New York: Friendship Press, 1955; London: World Dominion Press, 1955.

C.T. Studd: Cricketer and Pioneer, by Norman P. Grubb. London: Religious Tract Society, 1933.

Call to Istanbul, by Constance Padwick. London: Longmans, Green and Company, 1958.

Catch the Vision: The Story of HCJB—The Voice of the Andes. Opa Locka, Fla.: World Radio Missionary Fellowship, Inc., 1989.

A Chance to Die: The Life and Legacy of Amy Carmichael, by Elisabeth Elliot. Old Tappan, N.J.: Fleming H. Revell Company, 1987.

Christ in Congo Forests: The Story of the Heart of Africa Mission, by Norman Grubb. London: Lutterworth Press, 1945.

The Christ of the Indian Road, by E. Stanley Jones. New York & Cincinnati: Abingdon Press, 1925.

Christian World Mission, William K. Anderson, ed. Nashville: Commission on Ministerial Training, the Methodist Church, 1946.

"Church Growth Strategy Continued," by Donald McGavran in *International Review of Missions*, 1968.

Climbing: Memories of a Missionary's Wife, by Mrs. Jonathan Rosalind Goforth. Grand Rapids: Zondervan, 1940.

Come Up to This Mountain: The Miracle of Clarence W. Jones & HCJB, by Lois Neely. Wheaton, Ill.: Tyndale House Publishers, 1980.

Community Is My Language Classroom!, Tom and Betty Brewster, eds. Pasadena, Calif.: Lingua House Ministries, 1986.

David Livingstone, by J.H. Worcester, Jr. Chicago: Moody Press, 1987.

David Livingstone and Alexander Mackay: The Story of Their Lives, by B.K. Gregory and E.A. MacDonald. London: Sunday School Union, 1896.

The Disciplines of the Christian Life, by Eric Liddell. Nashville: Abingdon Press, 1985.

Dr. Ida: India: The Life-Story of Ida S. Scudder, by Mary Pauline Jeffery. New York: Fleming H. Revell Company, 1938.

Each One Teach One: Frank Laubach, Friend to Millions, by Marjorie Medary. New York: David McKay Company, 1954.

Eminent Missionary Women, by Mrs. J.T. Gracey. New York: Missionary Campaign Library (Eaton & Mains), 1898.

The Exile, by Pearl S. Buck. Reynal & Hitchcock, 1936.

The Flying Scotsman, by Sally Magnusson. New York: Quartet Books, 1981.

Fool & Fanatic? compiled by Jean Walker. Bucks (UK): Worldwide Evangelization Crusade, 1980.

A Foreign Devil in China: The Story of Dr. L. Nelson Bell, An American Surgeon in China, by John C. Pollock. Grand Rapids: Zondervan Publishing House (World Wide Publications), 1971.

Frank C. Laubach, Teacher of Millions, by David E. Mason. Minneapolis: T.S. Denison & Company, Inc., 1967.

From Jerusalem to Irian Jaya, by Ruth Tucker. Grand Rapids: The Zondervan Corporation, 1983.

George Grenfell: Pioneer in Congo, by H.L. Hemmens. London: Student Christian Movement, 1927.

Giants of the Missionary Trail. Chicago: Scripture Press Foundation, 1954.

Goforth of China, by Rosalind Goforth. Grand Rapids: Zondervan Publishing House, 1937.

The Gospel of Gentility: American Women Missionaries in Turn-of-the-Century China, by Jane Hunter. Boston: Yale University Press, 1984.

Great Christians, R.S. Forman, ed. London: Ivor Nicholson and Watson, 1933.

Great Missionaries: A Series of Biographies, by A. Thomson. New York: T. Nelson & Sons, 1862.

Great Missionaries to China. Grand Rapids: Zondervan Publishing House, 1947.

Guardians of the Great Commission, by Ruth Tucker. Grand Rapids: The Zondervan Corporation, 1988.

Henry Martyn, Saint and Scholar: First Modern Missionary to the Mohammedans, 1781-1812, by George Smith. Old Tappan, N.J.: Fleming H. Revell, n.d.

Heroes of Faith on Pioneer Trails, by E. Myers Harrison. Chicago: Moody Bible Institute, 1945.

Heroes of the Cross: Pandita Ramabai, Mary Slessor, Rasalama and Heroes in Madagascar. London: Marshall, Morgan, & Scott, Ltd., 1933.

How I Know God Answers Prayer: The Personal Testimony of One Lifetime, by Rosalind Goforth. Chicago: Moody Press, n.d.

Hudson Taylor and Maria: Pioneers in China, by John Pollock. New York: McGraw-Hill Book Co., Inc., 1962.

Hudson Taylor's Spiritual Secret, by Dr. & Mrs. Howard Taylor. Chicago: Moody Press, n.d.

In the Arena, by Isobel Kuhn. Singapore: Overseas Missionary Fellowship, 1960.

In the Gap: What It Means to Be a World Christian, by David Bryant. Inter-Varsity Christian Fellowship, U.S.A., 1979.

Ion Keith-Falconer of Arabia, by James Robson. London: Hodder & Stoughton, n.d.

Islam: A Challenge to Faith, by Samuel M. Zwemer. New York: Student Volunteer Movement for Foreign Missions, 1909.

Isobel Kuhn, by Lois Hoadley Dick. Minneapolis: Bethany House Publishers, 1987.

J. Hudson Taylor: A Man in Christ, by Roger Steer. Overseas Missionary Fellowship, n.d.

Johanna of Nigeria: Life and Labors of Johana Veenstra, S.U.M., by Henry Beets. Grand Rapids Printing Company, 1937.

Johnson of Nyasaland: A Study of the Life and Work of William Percival Johnson, D.D., by Bertram Herbert Barnes. Westminster: Universities' Mission to Central Africa, 1933.

The Journal of David Brainerd Vol. II. London: Andrew Melrose, 1902.

Jungle Pilot: The Life and Witness of Nate Saint, by Russell T. Hitt. New York: Harper & Brothers, 1959.

A Labrador Doctor: The Autobiography of Wilfred Thomason Grenfell. London: Hodder and Stoughton, n.d.

The Life of David Brainerd, Missionary to the Indians, by Jonathan Edwards. New York: The Christian Alliance Publishing Company, 1925.

The Life of Isabella Thoburn, by Bishop J.M. Thoburn. Cincinnati: Jennings and Pye, 1903.

The Life of William Carey, by Mary E. Farwell. Old Tappan, N.J.: Fleming H. Revell Company, 1888.

Livingstone the Pathfinder, by Basil Mathews. Missionary Movement of the United States and Canada, 1912.

Lord, Send Me! by Robert Savage. Grand Rapids: Zondervan Publishing House, 1943.

Malla Moe, by Maria Nilsen as told to Paul H. Sheetz. Chicago: Moody Bible Institute, 1956.

A Man Sent from God: A Biography of Robert E. Speer, by W. Reginald Wheeler. Old Tappan, N.J.: Fleming H. Revell Company, 1956.

Medical Missions at Work, by H.P. Thompson. Westminster: The Society for the Propagation of the Gospel in Foreign Parts, 1932.

Memoir of Mrs. Ann H. Judson, Late Missionary to Burmah, by James D. Knowles. Boston: Lincoln & Edmands, 1829.

A Memorial of the Futtehgurh Mission and her Martyred Missionaries, with some remarks on the Mutiny of India, by J. Johnston Walsh. Philadelphia: Joseph M. Wilson, 1859.

Men with the Heart of a Viking, by Douglas C. Percy. Alberta, Canada: Horizon House Publishers, 1976.

The Message of the Sermon on the Mount, by John R.W. Stott. Downers Grove, Ill.: Inter-Varsity Press, 1978.

Mission for Life: The story of the family of Adoniram Judson, the dramatic events of the first American foreign mission, and the course of evangelical religion in the nineteenth century, by Joan Jacobs Brumberg. New York: Free Press (Macmillan Publishing Co., 1980.

Missionary Crusaders for Christ, by Eugene Myers Harrison. Published by author, 1967.

Missionary Martyrs; being Brief Memorial Sketches of Faithful Servants of God Who Have Been Put to Death Whilst Endeavouring to Propagate the Gospel of Christ, Chiefly Among the Heathen, in Different Ages and Countries, by William Moister. London, 1885.

Missionary Principles, by Roland Allen. London: World Dominion Press, 1964.

Modern Heroes of the Mission Field, by W. Pakenham Walsh. London: Hodder & Stoughton, 1882.

Mountain Rain: A New Biography of James O. Fraser, by Eileen Crossman. Robensonia, Penn.: Overseas Missionary Fellowship, 1982.

Mountains Singing: The Story of Gospel Recordings in the Philippines, by Sanna Morrison Barlow. Chicago: Moody Press, 1960.

Much Prayer Much Power, by Peter Deyneka. Grand Rapids: Zondervan Publishing House, 1958.

Nests Above the Abyss, by Isobel Kuhn. Singapore: Overseas Missionary Fellowship, 1947.

The New Lottie Moon Story, by Catherine B. Allen. Nashville: Broadman Press, 1980.

Out of the Blanket: The Story of Sue and Kate McBeth, Missionaries to the Nez Perces, by Allen Conrad Morrill and Eleanor Dunlap Morrill. Idaho Research Foundation, Inc.: University Press of Idaho, 1978.

Pandita Ramabai: Her Vision, Her Mission and Triumph of Faith, by Helen S. Dyer. Edinburgh: Pickering & Inglis, n.d.

Pearls from Many Seas. Wheaton, Ill.: Van Kampen Press, 1951.

Pocket Prayers, by Robert C. Savage. Wheaton, Ill.: Tyndale House Publishers, 1982.

The Prayer of Faith, by J.O. Fraser. Kent, England: Overseas Missionary Fellowship, 1958.

Quaint Rhymes for the Battlefield, by C.T. Studd. London: James Clarke & Co., 1914.

Radio, the New Missionary, by Clarence W. Jones. Chicago: Moody Bible Institute, 1946.

Raymond Lull, the Illuminated Doctor: A Study in Mediaeval Missions, by W.T.A. Barber. London: Charles H. Kelly, n.d.

Recollections of Alexander Duff, and of the Mission College Which He Founded in Calcutta, by Lal Behari Day. London: T. Nelson and Sons, 1879.

Reform of the Ministry, by David Paton. London: Lutterworth Press, 1968.

Rejoicing in Christ: The Biography of Robert Carlton Savage, by Stephen E. Savage. Reading, Vermont: Shadow Rock Press, 1990.

Robert Moffat of Kuruman, by David J. Deane. Edinburgh: Pickering & Inglis, n.d.

Sacred Stories: Daily Devotions from the Family of God, by Ruth A. Tucker. Grand Rapids: Daybreak Books (Zondervan), 1989.

Servants of the King, by Robert E. Speer. Young People's Missionary Movement of the United States and Canada, 1909.

Shadow of the Almighty: The Life and Testament of Jim Elliot, by Elisabeth Elliot. New York: Harper & Row, 1958.

The Small Woman, by Alan Burgess. The Reprint Society of London, 1959.

The Smoke of a Thousand Villages . . . and Other Stories of Real Life Heroes of the Faith, by David and Naomi Shibley. Nashville: Thomas Nelson Publishers, 1989.

A Song of Ascents: a spiritual autobiography, by E. Stanley Jones. Festival ed. Nashville: Abingdon Press, 1979.

The Spontaneous Expansion of the Church, by Roland Allen. Grand Rapids: Eerdmans, 1962.

The Story of Dr. John G. Paton's Thirty Years with South Sea Cannibals, James Paton, ed. New York: George H. Doran Company, n.d.

The Story of Commander Allen Gardiner, R.N., with Sketches of Missionary Work in South America, by John W. Marsh and W.H. Stirling. London: James Nisbet & Co., 1887.

Student Mission Power. Pasadena, Calif.: William Carey Library, n.d.

T.J. Bach: A Voice for Missions, by Tom Watson, Jr. Chicago: Moody Press, 1965.

They Found the Secret, by V. Raymond Edman. Grand Rapids: Zondervan Publishing House, 1960.

They Were Pilgrims, by Marcus L. Loane. Sydney, Australia: Angus and Robertson, 1970.

Thinking Missions with Christ: Some Basic Aspects of World-Evangelism, Our Message, Our Motive and Our God, by Samuel M. Zwemer. Grand Rapids: Zondervan, 1935.

To Each Her Post: The Inspiring Lives of Six Great Women in China, by Phyllis Thompson. London: Hodder & Stoughton, 1982.

To the Golden Shore: The Life of Adoniram Judson, by Courtney Anderson. New York: Little Brown and Company, 1956.

The Transparent Woman, by Phyllis Thompson. Grand Rapids: Zondervan Publishing House, 1971.

The Triumph of John and Betty Stam, by Mrs. Howard Taylor. Chicago: Moody Press, 1935.

Uncle Cam: The Story of William Cameron Townsend, by James and Marti Hefley. Waco, Tex.: Word, Inc., 1974.

Understanding Church Growth, by Donald McGavran. Grand Rapids: Eerdmans, 1970.

The Unshakable Kingdom and the Unchanging Person, by E. Stanley Jones. Nashville: Abingdon Press, 1972.

Unstilled Voices, by James and Marti Hefley. Chappaqua, N.Y.: Christian Herald Books, 1981.

Victims of the Long March, by John Pollock. Waco, Tex.: Word Books, 1970.

Western Women in Eastern Lands, by Helen Barrett Montgomery. New York: the MacMillan Company, 1910.

When the Comforter Came: Thirty-one Meditations on the Holy Spirit—one for each day in the month, by A.B. Simpson. Harrisburg, Penn.: Christian Publications, 1911.

The White Queen of Okoyong: Mary Slessor, by W.P. Livingstone. London: Hodder & Stoughton, 1916.

Who Shall Ascend: The Life of R. Kenneth Strachan of Costa Rica, by Elisabeth Elliot. New York: Harper & Row, 1968.

William Carey: Missionary Pioneer and Statesman, by F. Deaville Walker. London: Student Christian Movement, 1926.

The World Their Household: The American Woman's Foreign Mission Movement and Cultural Transformation, 1870-1920, by Patricia R. Hill. University of Michigan Press, 1985.

"Wrong Strategy," by Donald McGavran in *International Review of Missions,* 1965.

You Heard It on HCJB, compiled by Nancy Woolnough. Quito, Ecuador: Vozandes Print Shop, 1975.

Index